▶ Goal Pursuit in Education Using Focused Action Research

List of previous publications by Eileen Piggot-Irvine
Books
Piggot-Irvine, E. (2009). *Action research in practice*. Wellington: NZCER.

Piggot-Irvine, E. & Bartlett, B. (2008). *Evaluating action research*. Wellington: NZCER.

Piggot-Irvine, E. & Cardno, C. (2005). *Appraising performance productively: Integrating accountability and development*. Auckland: Eversleigh Publishing.

Piggot-Irvine, E. & Gratton, R. (2005). *Action research: Stories from schools*. Auckland: Eversleigh Publishing.

Cardno, C. & Piggot-Irvine, E. (1997). *Effective performance appraisal: Integrating accountability and development in staff appraisal*. Auckland: Longman.

Book chapters
Piggot-Irvine, E. (forthcoming). Reflection. In D. Coghlan & M. Brydon-Miller (Eds.), *Encyclopedia of action research*. London: Sage.

Piggot-Irvine, E., Henwood, S., & Tosey, P. (2014). Introduction to leadership. In S. Henwood (Ed.), *Practical leadership in nursing and health care: A multi-professional approach* (pp. 1–18). Boca Raton, FL: CRC Press.

Piggot-Irvine, E. (2012). Creating authentic collaboration: A central feature of effectiveness. In O. Zuber-Skerritt (Ed.), *Action research for sustainable development in a turbulent world* (pp. 89–107). Bingley, UK: Emerald.

Piggot-Irvine, E. (2009). Action research as an approach to development. In E. Piggot-Irvine (Ed.), *Action research in practice* (pp. 11–30). Wellington: NZCER.

Piggot-Irvine, E. (2008). Introduction: What is evaluation of action research? In E. Piggot-Irvine & B. Bartlett (Eds.), *Evaluating action research* (pp. 9–52). Wellington: NZCER.

Piggot-Irvine, E. (2008). Meta-evaluation of action research in a school leadership programme. In E. Piggot-Irvine & B. Bartlett (Eds.), *Evaluating action research* (pp. 147–166). Wellington: NZCER.

Piggot-Irvine, E. (2008). Qualitative research methods for evaluating action research. In E. Piggot-Irvine & B. Bartlett (Eds.), *Evaluating action research* (pp. 53–90). Wellington: NZCER.

Piggot-Irvine, E. (1995). Reducing defensiveness by enhancing interpersonal effectiveness. In S. Pinchin & R. Passfield (Eds.), *Moving on: Creative applications of action learning and action research* (pp. 138–151). Brisbane: ALARPM Association.

Journal articles – refereed
Youngs, H. & Piggot-Irvine, E. (2014). The merits of triangulation: The evaluation of a New Zealand school leadership development program using mixed methods research. Method in Action Case Studies. *SAGE Research Methods Cases*. doi: http://dx.doi.org/10.1177/1558689811420696.

Piggot-Irvine, E., Howse, J., & Richard, V. (2013). South Africa principal role and development needs. *International Studies in Educational Administration*, 41(3), 55–72.

Rowe, W. E., Graf, M., Agger-Gupta, N., Piggot-Irvine, E., & Harris, B. (2013). Action research engagement: Creating the foundations for organizational change. Action Learning, Action Research Association, *Monograph Series*, 5.

Molyneux, C., Koo, N., Piggot-Irvine, E., Talmage, A., Travaglia, R., & Willis, M. (2012). Doing it together – collaborative research on goal-setting and review in a music therapy centre. *New Zealand Journal of Music Therapy*, 10, 6–38.

Piggot-Irvine, E. (2012). Tackling problems with staff necessitates deep leadership development. *Perspectives on Educational Leadership*, 4, Australian Council for Educational Leaders.

Plus 48 additional refereed papers. Please contact the author for full list.

palgrave▶pivot

Goal Pursuit in Education Using Focused Action Research

Eileen Piggot-Irvine
Program Head, MA-Leadership, Royal Roads University, Canada

palgrave
macmillan

GOAL PURSUIT IN EDUCATION USING FOCUSED ACTION RESEARCH
Copyright © Eileen Piggot-Irvine, 2015.
Foreword © Pip Bruce Ferguson, 2015.

All rights reserved.

First published in 2015 by
PALGRAVE MACMILLAN®
in the United States—a division of St. Martin's Press LLC,
175 Fifth Avenue, New York, NY 10010.

Where this book is distributed in the UK, Europe and the rest of the world, this is by Palgrave Macmillan, a division of Macmillan Publishers Limited, registered in England, company number 785998, of Houndmills, Basingstoke, Hampshire RG21 6XS.

Palgrave Macmillan is the global academic imprint of the above companies and has companies and representatives throughout the world.

Palgrave® and Macmillan® are registered trademarks in the United States, the United Kingdom, Europe and other countries.

ISBN: 978-1-137-50513-2 EPUB
ISBN: 978-1-137-50512-5 PDF
ISBN: 978-1-137-50511-8 Hardback

Library of Congress Cataloging-in-Publication Data is available from the Library of Congress.

A catalogue record of the book is available from the British Library.

First edition: 2015

www.palgrave.com/pivot

DOI: 10.1057/9781137505125

Contents

List of Figures	viii
List of Tables	ix
Foreword *Dr Pip Bruce Ferguson*	x
Acknowledgements	xii

1 Introduction to How a Reluctant Goal
  Pursuer Became Converted 1
  Inclinations for depth and collaborative
    processes 3
  Goal pursuit and alignment to other
    functions 8
  What this book does not and does cover 10
  Summary 12

2 Why Should You Engage in Goal Pursuit? 13
  Introduction 14
  Why have goals? 14
  Importance of goals in education 15
  Importance of goals in the
    non-education sector 17
  Links to recent research from neuroscience
    and neuroleadership 20
  Another view on this neuroscience and
    neuroleadership material linked to goals 28
  My cautionary note 28
  Summary 30

Contents

3	**A Simple, Yet Detailed, Model for Goal Pursuit**	31
	Introduction	32
	Background to AR as the core of the FAR model for goal pursuit	32
	The FAR model	33
	Recommendations for further improvement and reporting achievement	52
	Summary	56
4	**How the FAR Model Encourages Shift in Depth, Lift in Challenge, and Collaboration**	57
	Introduction	58
	'Shift in depth' in goal pursuit	58
	'Lift' in goal pursuit	61
	Authentic collaboration and feedback	65
	Summary	75
5	**What This Looks Like in a Real Case Study**	76
	Introduction	77
	Case study	77
	How the meta-level case stacked up against research and neuroleadership thinking	83
	Summary	87
6	**Ten Useful Activities, Tools and Templates**	88
	Introduction	89
	Activity 1: clarifying principles for goal pursuit for your organization	89
	Activity 2: aligning, cascading, goals in Preparatory phase	90
	Activity 3: brainstorming 'literature review' ideas to become 'informed' in the Reconnaissance phase	91
	Activity 4: planning for collecting data for Reconnaissance phase in the FAR Model	93
	Activity 5: summarizing findings from the Reconnaissance phase in the FAR Model	93
	Activity 6: planning for the Implementation phase in the FAR Model	94

Activity 7: evaluation of Implementation phase activity   97
Activity 8: GAS as a specific Evaluation phase activity   97
Activity 9: ensuring ownership of the findings and
    recommendations through FFA   98
Activity 10: reflecting on Evaluation phase findings
    and reporting   100

References   102

Index   109

List of Figures

1.1	Eileen in a non-constrained mode	2
1.2	The front cover of *Appraising Performance Productively*	4
1.3	Focused Action Research (FAR) Model for goal pursuit	7
1.4	Aligning goals enhances performance	10
2.1	Prefrontal region of the brain	22
2.2	Low stress, positive emotion, and reward conditions	23
2.3	Conditions creating approach response in goal pursuit	26
3.1	Cascading of goals	35
3.2	Force Field Analysis diagram	53
4.1	Balancing advocacy and inquiry	69
4.2	Graphic representation of deepening levels of interactive challenge in collaboration	72
5.1	The FAR Model in School A	78
5.2	Cascading of goals in School A	79
6.1	Cascading goals for your own organization	91
6.2	Brainstorming literature review topics	92

List of Tables

3.1	Selected data collection methods	40
3.2	Sean's deep action plan—Reconnaissance and Implementation phases	44
3.3	Sean's Evaluation phase activity	48
3.4	GAS for use with Sean's plans	50
3.5	Advantages and disadvantages of GAS ratings	51
4.1	An example of a deep level plan	62
4.2	Deepening levels of interactive challenge in collaboration	71
4.3	Dialogue steps for achieving authentic collaboration	74
5.1	GAS use at a meta-level in School A	81
5.2	School A goal pursuit match to key neuroleadership elements	86
6.1	Principles underpinning leading and implementation of goal pursuit	90
6.2	Locating key literature or other reference sources	92
6.3	Data collection for Reconnaissance phase	93
6.4	Analysis and reflection upon the Reconnaissance results	93
6.5	Deep level plan: Template 1	95
6.6	Deep level plan: Template 2	96
6.7	Planning for Evaluation phase data collection	97
6.8	GAS for use with your own deep plan	98
6.9	FFA process steps	99
6.10	Reflecting and reporting on results	100
6.11	Final report writing outline for overall project	101

Foreword

Leaders in education today are faced with difficult situations. They are pressured by political directives, high expectations from governments, community, students, and parents, and the requirement to do more and more with less and less, and in the midst of all this to maintain or extend their own levels of competence. How can they achieve this?

Eileen Piggot-Irvine is a researcher, teacher, and author who has consistently sought to help. I have worked with her on projects to recognize excellence in the induction of new teachers, in evaluation of professional development projects for teachers of indigenous students in mainstream schools, and in the development of aspiring principals. Eileen and I share the same passion for using action research to improve our own practice and to help others see how they might improve theirs. We share a common background of decades of experience in staff development.

This latest book provides a wealth of synthesized knowledge from Eileen's extensive experience in coaching educational leaders, academics, and students. While building soundly on existing literature—and introducing the new field of neuroscience and its relevance—she provides models and advice to help education leaders with the task of co-developing appropriate goals with those they lead. The book is expressed in direct and simple language. It includes regular 'pauses for reflection' where readers are encouraged to think about how the content challenges or reinforces their own previous experience.

A hallmark of Eileen's practice has always been her searing honesty about improving her own practice, and offering advice from past experience that might help others to avoid the 'holes in the sidewalk' that can be negotiated with judicious assistance. She speaks to the reader in the first person, populating her chapters with excellent diagrams, down-to-earth case studies, and useful summaries. I have found typical of her style, when working with her, the qualities that she encourages in this book: clear demonstration of lengthy and thoughtful engagement with her field; alerting the reader to the importance of values, not just needs, in goal pursuit activity; exhibiting care in the declaration of possible partiality of perspectives; maintaining an open and critical view of both strengths and criticisms of action research and how it might be strengthened through her FAR model; an approach to skill-building that relies on scaffolding to support busy leaders and students; and a variety of tools, activities, and templates to help readers to implement the ideas in the book.

Eileen knows what it is to work in the morass of busy, pressured educational institutions. She provides sound practical advice to help others to pursue clear, collaborative, achievable goals in their educational organizations. I warmly recommend this book to readers seeking such help.

Dr Pip Bruce Ferguson
Teaching Enhancement Unit
Dublin City University, Ireland

Acknowledgements

There are many people I would like to thank who have supported this book. First and foremost, Principal A and her school have been extremely generous in providing permission to be a case study in this book. The willingness to grow that has been shown at individual and collective level in this school has been extraordinary and I feel blessed to have been associated with them over several years. As somewhat of a 'footnote', the school has recently been externally reviewed and received an excellent report for all aspects of leadership, development, and innovation. Some of the steps Principal A and her leadership team took that led to this outcome are outlined in this book.

Second, I wish to thank Julie Brown, a mid-career teacher, who took time out of her holiday to read, critique, and offer suggestions for making this book more attractive to teachers. Julie's expertise in reconstructing the model introduced in this book has been deeply appreciated.

I am deeply indebted to Pip Bruce Ferguson, a special, critical friend, for the generosity she always shows in providing clear and honest feedback. She also helped to set the tone for this book in the Foreword.

I also want to pay due respect and gratitude to Jane Culhane. As an extraordinary principal she has provided wonderful feedback on the relevance, structure, and content of this book. Jane is just one of a multitude of education sector leaders that I have introduced to goal pursuit but she is, and always has been, an outstanding supporter of this work.

I want to acknowledge Joan King (sadly deceased in 2014), neuroscientist, who provided wisdom and insight in my journey of fathoming out the neuroscience underpinnings of neuroleadership claims. I am yet to meet a more generous academic.

Finally, I wish to deeply and sincerely thank all the principals, leaders, teachers, and students from amazing schools and other educational organizations I have had the privilege to work with. Without these people, and particularly those who have pushed me to record what I have done with them, this book would never have been written.

palgrave▸pivot

www.palgrave.com/pivot

1
Introduction to How a Reluctant Goal Pursuer Became Converted

Abstract: Chapter 1 backgrounds my interest and rationale for goal pursuit: an interest that was far from enthusiastic at the beginning of my career. The importance of goal pursuit for strategic planning, development, learning, and performance review is discussed. A particular focus is placed on how alignment of goals in strategic planning and performance review can enhance performance. This chapter also outlines how I have translated my interest in action research (AR) to the Focused Action Research (FAR) Model for goal pursuit. Brief details of this simple model and associated phased activity are introduced; the rest of the book elaborates this activity. The FAR Model encourages evidence-based phases of Preparation, Reconnaissance, Implementation, Evaluation, Recommendation drawing, and Reporting in goal pursuit. It is underpinned by the three key principles of shift in depth, lift in challenge, and authentic collaboration.

Keywords: action research; authentic collaboration; challenge; depth; FAR Model; goal alignment; performance review

Piggot-Irvine, Eileen. *Goal Pursuit in Education Using Focused Action Research.* New York: Palgrave Macmillan, 2015. DOI: 10.1057/9781137505125.0006.

In my career as a teacher, leader, and coach to hundreds of leaders in almost every type of organization I have often heard people speaking disdainfully about focusing on goal pursuit (which I am defining as goal setting, achievement, and evaluation). I have listened to many people resisting the thought of being constrained by goals, rather favouring to enjoy being a free spirit and letting patterns, work, and life unfold in serendipitous ways. I confess I have a strong element of that in my own personality too, so I have some sympathy with the sentiment.

FIGURE 1.1   *Eileen in a non-constrained mode*

Early in my career, I clearly recall a neighbour, a professional woman, asking what my plans A, B, and C were for my career direction. I remember being dumbstruck. I felt deeply disturbed at the thought of being so tightly pinned down and in many ways I have not changed in that feeling. Although I am doggedly determined and focused (or many would say "stubborn") in whatever I pursue, I have not favoured narrow, long-term planning. My career, for example, has unwrapped like one of those beautifully layered parcels with a precious surprise in the middle.

If I had been following plan A, B, or C, I would never have reached that gem in the middle which I usually describe as my perfect role.

So, given this sentiment, you may well ask why on earth I would choose to write a book on goal pursuit! I think the answer to this lies in my cumulative experience rather than in my somewhat independent spirit. As a leader and coach (and mother), I have sometimes been painfully reminded that not everyone, including myself, finds it easy to either select or focus on goals through to full pursuit. It is within these roles, and to resolve my own reluctance to formalize pursuit of goals, that I have realized the need to create an approach to goal pursuit fitting my own inclinations. These inclinations, especially in my professional life, include favouring depth and evidence rather than superficiality and subjectivity, doing fewer things well, a fascination with action research (AR) and improvement oriented processes, and an emphasis on authentic collaboration.

Inclinations for depth and collaborative processes

The content of this book reflects my inclinations but it also results from a couple of decades of development. I started practising the approaches to goal pursuit outlined in this book in my first leadership role where I was tasked with creating an 'appraisal', performance review, system for an educational organization. I spent months struggling with reviewing the literature on effectiveness in this field in order to consolidate my thinking on how a system could be developmental yet meet organizational accountability needs. Despite my aversion to tight goal setting, I kept circling back to the necessity of strongly owned yet meaningful and explicit goals. I developed a system which centred on goals that were personally relevant and developmentally deep whilst strategically aligned at the organization level (Piggot-Irvine, 2003). I introduced this system with work teams I led with reasonable success, to the extent that others from outside the organization frequently asked me to facilitate sessions on the topic or help design their own approach.

The system I introduced led to the book *Appraising Performance Productively* (Piggot-Irvine & Cardno, 2005) for the education sector, which had a particular interest around the goal pursuit elements, and it sold like hotcakes. Subsequently, I have continued to strengthen my thinking about goal pursuit and appraisal/performance review and written more than ten articles associated with this topic, in addition to implementing presentations and workshops with hundreds of leaders within my consultancy and teaching practice. More and more frequently I have received requests to share my recent research, thinking, and tools with those who struggle either with goal pursuit for themselves or with guiding staff in this arena. This book outlines what I have developed and shared with others.

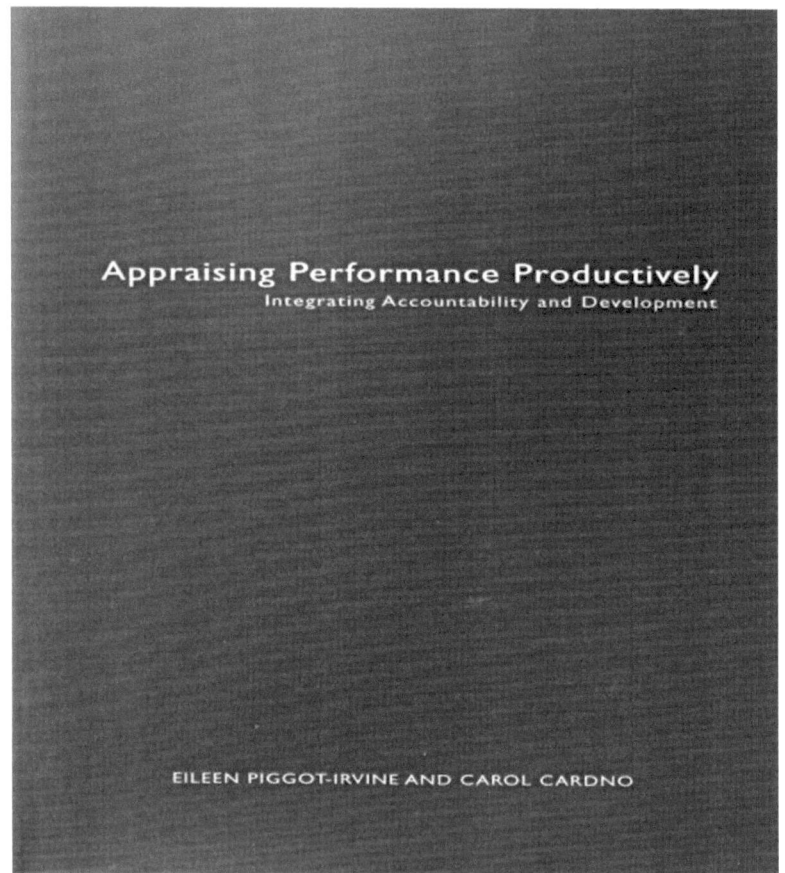

FIGURE 1.2   *The front cover of* Appraising Performance Productively

I have alluded to some inclinations and interests which have strongly influenced my approach to goal pursuit, and although each is elaborated further in later chapters, I just want to highlight a couple as an introduction. In the earliest stages of my career I was a biologist and you will see the objective biologist in me has never totally disappeared. It shows up in this book in my emphasis on encouraging evidence- or data-based decision making. I constantly search for verification for any viewpoint or assumption. Similarly, as a biologist, lately I have become fascinated with what we are learning about the brain's response to stimuli. I have narrowed my interest in this 'neuroscience' field to searching for what is known about goal pursuit and brain response. I present a slightly cautious, 'amber-light', view on the way the more popularized neuroleadership field is presenting the results of this neuroscience research. However, the biologist in me could not resist including some of this material, because even though we know relatively little about how the brain works, many of the ideas drawn by the neuroleadership proponents actually fit very well with my own experience with goal pursuit.

A further interest, passion, that comes through strongly in the book is that of a 20-year obsession with an AR orientation in my approach to research and development (Piggot-Irvine, 2012; Piggot-Irvine & Bartlett, 2008; Piggot-Irvine, 2009; Piggot-Irvine, Connelly, Curry, Hanna, Moodie, Palmer, Peri, & Thompson, 2011). In this approach, as the name suggests, there is intent to move beyond just data collection to ensuring that change and improvement follows this data collection or research. In the AR approach I have adopted, an initial Preparatory focusing phase is followed by a 'Reconnaissance' or informed current situation analysis phase of activity, then 'Implementation' of improvement associated with the focus, 'Evaluation' of achievement, creation of Recommendations, and Reporting the findings, and then links are created to further improvement. I have incorporated this iterative, or cycled, phased activity for the context of evidence-based goal pursuit in the Focused Action Research (FAR) Model, a model underpinning much of the content of this book. The Model phases (which are detailed in Chapter 3) cover the following range of activities:

Preparatory

- clarifying principles underpinning goal pursuit
- setting priorities at a national or governance level
- selecting goals to match priorities
- allocating of resources to goals

Reconnaissance

- collecting data/evidence on the current situation in terms of practices (and gaps) associated with the goal

- gathering information (literature, previous research, etc.) on effective practice with the topic
- drawing conclusions about where improvement is needed
- planning for improvement steps, with clear timelines and measurable outcomes

Implementation

- carrying out the planned improvements
- recording reflections on implementation as it progresses

Evaluation/Review

- collecting data/evidence on achievement of improvement steps
- drawing conclusions about where further improvement is needed

Recommendations and Reporting

- presenting and reporting findings
- drawing up recommendations with key influencers in the organization

Further Improvement

- planning further improvement associated with goal.

Each of the activities listed here is also depicted in Figure 1.3. You will notice that there is a 'spin-off' cycle depicted in the Model. McNiff (1988) argues that we need to allow for dealing with more than one issue at a time, or one issue raising further issues, and this is typical of what we have experienced in AR.

Underpinning the FAR Model are three key principles:

- creating a shift in 'depth' in goals;
- ensuring challenge (or 'lift'); and
- engaging in authentic collaboration in goal pursuit.

Although each of the underpinnings is outlined in detail in Chapter 4, I will briefly introduce these principles here.

Shift in 'depth' with goal pursuit is linked to multiple factors. Depth is indicated when goals are written or articulated at a level which begins by creating a thorough, evidence-based exploration of both current practice and best practice theory/research associated with a goal topic (a 'Reconnaissance' activity) prior to embarking on any ideas for improvement. It also includes utilizing evidence, or data, in decision making and

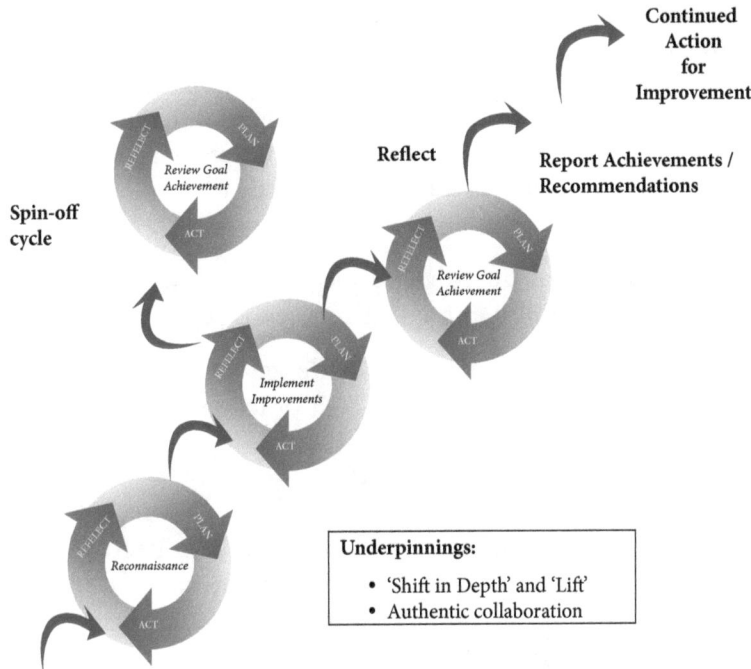

FIGURE 1.3 *Focused Action Research (FAR) Model for goal pursuit*
Source: Adapted from Piggot-Irvine, 2002.

evaluation at varied points in the goal pursuit process. 'Depth' and AR are intricately linked.

'Lift' in challenge, the second key principle underpinning the FAR Model associated with goal pursuit, is of equal importance. This is more significant at the early, goal selection, stage of goal pursuit. Low-level order challenge, easy-to-achieve goals, in my observation, generally create low-level outcomes. In contrast, high-level expectations with more specific and demanding goals are usually associated with a level of challenge or 'lift'.

Authentic collaboration, the third underpinning principle of the FAR Model, is a principle with impact on every single activity in goal pursuit and is critical to its success. Collaboration is what creates enhancement of 'buy-in', or ownership, by both those leading and those influenced by goal pursuit. 'Authentic collaboration' (Piggot-Irvine, 2012) is a term encompassing multiple levels of activity associated with the importance of engaging in genuine 'dialogue' that is respectful and supports 'productive', courageous, rather than 'defensive' interactions.

> Think about goal pursuit you have been involved in and respond to the following questions:
>
> ▸ To what extent was there an evidence-based exploration of both current practice and best practice theory/research associated with a goal topic before embarking on ideas for improvement?
>
> ▸ How would you describe the level of challenge; that is, were the goals easy to achieve or more specific and demanding goals? If the latter, were the outcomes enhanced by such 'lift'?
>
> ▸ How collaborative was the goal pursuit? Did key players engage in genuine 'dialogue' that was non-defensive? If so, how do you think that collaboration influenced buy-in for the goal pursuit?

Goal pursuit and alignment to other functions

Goal pursuit is not a single-purpose activity associated only with strategic planning or development or learning. As mentioned earlier in this introduction, it is central also to performance review (also called 'appraisal' in many countries). All of these functions are linked, but the linkage is especially tight between strategic planning and performance review. That linkage is noted clearly in the FAR Model for goal pursuit, where the importance of alignment and cascading in selection of goals is indicated. I am always surprised when leaders have not thought about the importance of aligned strategic and performance review goals. In fact, I would estimate that approximately 80 per cent of leaders I have worked with have needed to be alerted to that link, a link they have not previously thought of.

> *I am always surprised when leaders have not thought about the importance of aligned strategic and performance review goals.*

Much of my thinking about the FAR Model, shifting to deep goals, lifting challenge, and creating authentic collaboration, is derived from my early work in performance review (Piggot-Irvine, 1996; Piggot-Irvine, 2003; Piggot-Irvine & Cardno, 2005) rather than the specific goal pursuit context. Although it is not a central focus of this book, I want to be explicit about my belief that performance review should have a developmental goal pursuit purpose which is equal to the common 'accountability' intent of this human resource activity. I have been employed as the performance reviewer for more than 130 leaders and where this dual purpose is employed I have never experienced derision or discontent with the approach.

It seems to me that ensuring an equal development or improvement purpose in performance review which is associated with a 'growth mindset' is the key to ensuring this is a valued and valuable process. Previously (Piggot-Irvine, 2003), I have described the dual performance review purpose as leading to "an integrated development and accountability approach" (p. 76). Central to the 'development' component of this dual purpose is a goal pursuit approach which closely mirrors that outlined in the FAR Model.

Specific, individualized, development goal alignment to team and organization goals is equally important in both performance review and goal pursuit as processes. In other words, the cascading of goals described later in Chapter 3 applies also in performance review goal pursuit. Further, the phased activities of Reconnaissance, Implementation, and Evaluation can also be followed, and the underpinning principles of shift in depth, lift, and authentic collaboration are foundational to performance review. I am always concerned when leaders see performance review goal setting as detached from general goal pursuit, with a consequence of multiple unaligned goal pursuit activity which creates excessive, unnecessary work for employees and considerable waste of resources. A critical task for an organization is to align performance review with all other types of goal pursuit activity, as shown in Figure 1.4.

[Strategic Goals] → [Performance Review Goals] → [Enhanced Organizational and Individual Performance]

FIGURE 1.4 *Aligning goals enhances performance*

What this book does not and does cover

Before outlining the content of the book, I should also point out what this book does *not* intend to do! There is minimal coverage of the history or alternative models of goal pursuit in this book. These interesting topics are well covered in multiple other books and a simple Google search will produce a wealth of such background material. Locke and Latham's (2013) recent book, for example, is an invaluable resource for this background.

Instead, I have focused in this book on an AR model for goal pursuit, which is somewhat new for the field. The incorporation of some neuroscience and neuroleadership thinking into this AR model also differs from other writing and practice beyond the neuroleadership field itself. Further, one particular tool for gathering evidence in the Evaluation phase in the FAR Model introduced in this book is Goal Attainment Scaling (GAS). This tool is virtually unknown in the goal pursuit field and therefore is also new thinking.

This brief introductory description of activities in the AR goal pursuit approach provides a platform for fuller elaboration in each subsequent chapter of the book. I want to note from the outset that I have deliberately chosen to focus on the education context when illustrating concepts associated with the FAR Model for goal pursuit. Though I have also worked in the non-education context as a consultant with goal pursuit, it is the school sector that has fascinated me, particularly in terms of the age range the goal pursuit context applies to, that is young to older students through to employees. In one school, for example, the goals of a class of six-year-olds were displayed on the walls of the classroom.

Chapter 2 covers the rationale for setting goals, whether for leaders, staff, or learners. Links are drawn between findings of previous researchers on achievement and goal pursuit and the FAR Model. In this chapter, I also make links to recent evidence from neuroscience and neuroleadership as rationale for goal pursuit and to provide a little insight into activity shown in the brain to encourage good goal pursuit. As I have mentioned earlier, conclusions on the popularized neuroleadership material may not always be shown as strongly evidenced because the neuroscience field is very new; however, much of the neuroleadership interpretation of this material fits strongly with my own experience.

In Chapter 3, the FAR Model is described in detail. The chapter begins with backgrounding AR as the core of the Model. The 'action' and 'research' dual purposes are described as well as opinion on the relevance of this approach. Each of the Preparatory, Reconnaissance, Implementation/intervention, Evaluation, Recommendations and Reporting phases of the Model are then outlined alongside examples of implementation in schools. A distinct section of this chapter is associated with discussion of GAS as a tool for self-, peer, or group evaluation in goal pursuit. This tool is virtually unknown outside the counselling, care, and psychology sectors, yet it has been exceptionally well received when I have introduced it with goal pursuit in other sectors.

In Chapter 4, the three underpinning principles of the FAR Model are discussed. The rationale for 'shift' in depth and 'lift' in challenge is offered, followed by a more detailed elaboration of 'authentic collaboration' as a central feature of effective goal pursuit. The latter, I believe, is considerably overlooked in discussion of goal pursuit in other publications, yet it is the underpinning which I consider to hold more significance to success than any other element. Specifically, in this section I attempt to show not only the defensive strategies and values preventing authentic collaboration but also what can be 'productively' implemented to enhance it.

Chapter 5 provides a case study illustrating the way the FAR Model for goal pursuit has been practised in one school. The case study is one of the best examples demonstrating all of the phases of the FAR Model. It is not a highly sophisticated or perfect example (these do not exist), but shows a real application context. In all honesty, though many schools I have worked with have attempted multiple components of the FAR Model, I have rarely experienced a full-blown dedication to all elements. For example, most of these schools have implemented up to the Evaluation phase well but I have found it exceptionally difficult to get a progression to collecting evaluation data before the principal has substantially moved on to focusing on new goals. I have considerable concern about such lack of emphasis on Evaluation as a confirming, consolidating, phase of the Model because not only is the chance to show invaluable evidence of successful implementation and achievement missed, so is celebration of achievement and most importantly clarification about next steps for improvement being well-informed. This chapter concludes with discussion of reporting on goal pursuit.

Chapter 6 includes activities, tools, and templates for goal pursuit outlined in the book. I have ordered the activities to match the phases in the FAR Model for goal pursuit. I am currently strengthening the employment of GAS and can report that once users get beyond the establishment of categories for ratings in the GAS table, they not only find it easy to use after the first attempt, but also report positively on the wealth of dialogue created when the ratings are discussed. I offer these activities for use within your own schools.

Finally, a comment on the tone and layout of this book; it is what I would describe as semi-academic. I need to declare I have a strong need for a research, evidence, backup in my work, but I also attempt to articulate my thinking and tools in a way which is hopefully still readable to those who are not pure academics. My career has always bridged the academic and practitioner worlds, and my writing attempts the same. I hope you find this approach useful.

Summary

- Goal pursuit is important for strategic planning, development, learning, performance review and so on.
- Alignment of goals in strategic planning and performance review can enhance performance.
- The FAR Model encourages focused, evidence-based phases of Reconnaissance, Implementation, Evaluation, Recommendations, and Reporting in goal pursuit.
- The FAR Model encourages shift in depth, lift in challenge, and authentic collaboration.

2
Why Should You Engage in Goal Pursuit?

Abstract: *Chapter 2 begins by covering why everyone in schools and the wider education context should consider goal pursuit, whether leaders, staff, or learners. Links are drawn between the FAR Model and findings of previous researchers on goal pursuit. In this chapter, I also make links to recent evidence from neuroscience and neuroleadership as rationale for goal pursuit and to provide some insight into activity shown in the brain to encourage good goal pursuit. In particular, the response of the prefrontal cortex (PFC) in conditions of low (approach) and high (avoid) threat and stress is discussed. Conclusions from the popularized neuroleadership material are critiqued because this field is very new and its claims are not always well evidenced in terms of research. Despite this caution however I discuss how much of the neuroleadership interpretation of this material fits strongly with my own experience on good goal pursuit.*

Keywords: neuroleadership; neuroscience; research on the rationale for goal pursuit

Piggot-Irvine, Eileen. *Goal Pursuit in Education Using Focused Action Research.* New York: Palgrave Macmillan, 2015. DOI: 10.1057/9781137505125.0007.

Introduction

A loose interpretation of Locke and Latham's (2006) definition of a goal is an aim that we seek to achieve or obtain. Goal setting involves the conscious process of establishing levels of performance in order to obtain desirable outcomes. The broader term goal pursuit, however, encompasses all elements of goal setting, planning, implementation, achievement and monitoring. As Ferguson and Porter (2010) suggest, "... one of the hallmark characteristics of goal pursuit is its inherent intentional and conscious planning, execution, and monitoring" (p. 313). The broader arena of goal pursuit is the focus of this book. In this chapter, the rationale and importance for having both personal and organizational goals is provided with links made to the FAR Model. This is followed by a discussion of the rationale for goal pursuit derived from neuroscience research and writing.

Why have goals?

Goals are often considered to be linked to personal and organizational meaning in life and described as helping us to focus. As Vorhauser-Smith (2011) states:

> ... goals provide an end point or target, against which we can determine performance – successful or otherwise. We aspire to goal achievement – goals represent our progress over time and when achieved, provide a sense of completion and satisfaction. In this way, goals are integral to giving meaning and purpose to our lives. (p. 6)

Vorhauser-Smith gives considerable credence to the importance of goals in this statement. She implies that the sense of completion, personal satisfaction and meaning we get from goal pursuit is linked to motivation. As early as in 1968, Locke, perhaps the most prolific writer/researcher about goals, had also reported that working towards a goal was a source of personal work motivation. It is important to note the close link between motivation and self-regulation because motivation is enhanced when rewards are maximized and threat is minimized. Leithwood, Aitken and Jantzi (2006) make this motivation link more explicit. They summarize that not just any random goal will enhance motivation and suggest goals must be personally compelling, challenging, and achievable. Challenging goals, they contest, can raise a person's self-efficacy. It can be concluded from Vorhauser-Smith and the Leithwood et al. thinking that goals should have meaningfulness and be seen to create meaning.

Importance of goals in education

The role of goal pursuit in engaging students in learning is a distinctive element in the education sector literature. 'Engagement' is often seen to occur when students make a personal investment in their learning and take pride in accomplishing learning objectives (Gordon, 2006). The latter 'learning objectives' component implies a practice of goal pursuit.

Current international research on student learning and leadership of learning indicates a multitude of influences associated with student and staff achievement and these range from person-centred conditioned influences through to broader leadership, team, organizational, and environmental elements. Despite the multitude of influences, there is a consistent message in material on educational achievement and organizational effectiveness in this sector related to the importance of setting goals for attaining direction at both the personal and organizational level. The Institute for Education Leadership (IEL) in Ontario (2011), for example, rated most highly the significance on achievement of influences such as: setting goals; aligning resources with priorities; using data; engaging in courageous conversations; and promoting collaborative learning cultures. All items in the IEL list are directly linked to goal pursuit in the way it is outlined in this book.

> *There is a consistent message in educational achievement and organizational effectiveness material related to the importance of setting goals for attaining direction at both the personal and organizational level.*

'Setting goals' is a fairly generalized description which I am interpreting as including 'selecting' goals as a preface activity to clarifying, articulating, recording, implementing and evaluating goals. In the FAR Model outlined in this book, such selecting goals activity initiates the cycle. The emphasis placed on this by IEL indicates just how important the early, Preparatory phase, activity is to goal pursuit.

'Aligning resources with priorities' is also explicitly stated in the FAR Model. You will also note that 'using data' features on the IEL list and this evidence-based, informed component of goal pursuit is highlighted in the FAR Model as an essential feature of both the Reconnaissance and Evaluation phases. Additionally, the IEL prioritizing of 'promoting collaborative learning cultures' and 'engaging in courageous conversations' links directly to an underpinning key principle of authentic collaboration noted for the FAR Model.

Robinson, Hohepa and Lloyd (2009) have continued to underscore the importance of goal pursuit by ranking 'establishing goals and expectations' as first amongst eight key dimensions for leadership in the school sector. They note this 'establishing goals and expectations' label they assign to goal pursuit at an organization level includes:

- setting;
- communicating;
- monitoring learning goals, standards, and expectations; and
- the involvement of staff and others in the process for clarity and consensus about goals.

If we unpack this list, the 'setting' goals element links to the 'Reconnaissance' phase activity in the FAR Model. The 'monitoring' elements are aligned to 'Evaluation' phase activity, and the 'communicating', 'clarity', and 'consensus' elements directly link to the underpinning key principle of authentic collaboration in the Model.

Reiterating support for goal pursuit, Leithwood and Reihl (2003) further suggest that 'setting directions' in an organization is a core practice of effective educational leadership. 'Providing direction' is one of the features at the heart of leadership according to these authors. I interpret that Leithwood and Reihl are covering all of the elements of goal pursuit when they describe both setting and providing direction therefore their statements offer support for such activity.

> Think about goal pursuit you have been involved in and respond to the following questions.
>
> - What has been the purpose of the goal pursuit you have engaged in?
>
> - Which elements of 'goal pursuit' (goal selection, clarifying, articulating, recording, implementing, evaluating) were emphasized in your engagement?
>
> - If a low level or engagement in full goal pursuit is apparent in your school, what do you think the reasons for that might be?

Despite the strong rationale for goal pursuit in schools provided by many authors, Conzemius and O'Neill (2006) remind us that goal setting has yet to become real and compelling in schools at either a personal or organizational level. There may be multiple reasons for this situation, some perhaps linked to my earlier reference in Chapter 1 to the resistance many feel when they think they are being constrained by tightly locked-in pursuit of goals. Another reason for goal setting not being compelling could be associated with the autonomous nature of the role of a teacher. Most teachers have considerable independence inside their own classroom and enjoy the freedom to work with some degree of autonomy in their approaches to teaching. Being asked to set specific goals is likely to be seen as an affront to such autonomy by those who treasure their independence. Equally, however, I am observing many teachers increasingly seeing the importance of both transparency and alignment of content in teaching and learning. I would conclude there is a shift towards greater acceptance of the importance of goal pursuit in both teaching and student learning. A further reason for goal setting not to be compelling in the education sector could be linked to leaders, teachers and learners not having sufficient knowledge and tools for goal pursuit itself. This book hopefully provides some of the latter.

Importance of goals in the non-education sector

Although this book is focused on the education sector, it is interesting to examine whether a similar theme is evident in the literature of setting and providing direction as an important element to leadership in organizations. Kouzes and Posner (2007), for example, offer quite a generalized description of goal pursuit but also stress its importance to achievement. These exceptionally well reported researchers and authors in leadership suggest that leaders should expect the best by holding high and clear expectations and goals for the organization. Latham (2004), another well published researcher and author on goal pursuit, offers that goals are seen to inspire individuals, assist with self-management, provide purpose and challenge, and that they may result in motivation to explore new knowledge as well as enhanced pride in work. As a further argument for goal pursuit, Asplund and Blacksmith (2013) have reported when goals are set based on personal strengths, employees were seven times more likely to be high performers.

There are several determinants of effective achievement in goal pursuit noted in the non-education sector. Locke and Latham (2013), for example, underscore the significance of the collaborative element when emphasizing the importance of feedback around individual goals—particularly personalizing recognition and feedback. This feedback element is further supported by Cummings and Worely (2009) who suggest that employees need continual feedback in order to achieve goals. In Chapter 4, extensive elaboration of the feedback and collaboration link to the FAR Model is provided.

Several authors reiterate the importance of cascading and alignment of personal through to organizational goals—a crucial Preparatory phase activity in the FAR Model—yet one I have not seen well implemented in organizations generally. My experience is confirmed by Kaplan and Norton (2001) who issue a sobering message when stating only approximately seven percent of employees understand what is expected of them to achieve company goals. Organizational goals need to be clearly explained (Locke & Latham, 2002) when presented by leaders. Getting employees to accept and understand organizational goals, however, is no easy task. These cascading and alignment issues in the education sector are discussed in more detail in Chapter 3.

Uhl-Bein and Marion (2009) indicate the importance to engagement of the interdependence of employee needs and expectations and higher level organizational goals. They articulate this well in the following quote: "Shared need instead starts with the 'what's in it for me?' question and whether it is advantageous to work together to accomplish personal goals; it understands that if interdependence is not inherent or acknowledged, the likelihood of fully engaging others is slim" (p. 642).

I want to extend this latter point a little. I have noted with interest what meagre attention is paid in the goal pursuit material to matching values, rather than just needs, in goal setting activity. Exceptions though can be found in the work of Snyder and Lopez (2005) who suggest that goals should to be tied to values, i.e. to what is important to the organization and individuals. Sheldon (2002) also stresses the importance of 'self-concordance' by people selecting goals which are meaningful and link to individual values in goal pursuit.

I think there needs to be greater emphasis on this values-linking. From a very personal perspective, if I reflect on the goals that have been most inspiring, it is those goals which have led to the most significant sense of achievement and fulfilment. They genuinely provided me with meaning in life, a target, and the associated deep sense of satisfaction referred to by Vorhauser-Smith (2011). They have been personally compelling, challenging, and achievable and hugely raised my self-efficacy, as also noted by Leithwood, Aitken, and Jantzi (2006). They sustained me in a couple of turbulent and isolated times, as well as opening up some extraordinary collaborative relationships. Put simply, I believe that people need to see meaning in goals—at an organizational as well as individual level.

> ... if I reflect on the goals that have been most inspiring to me, it is those goals which have led to the most significant sense of achievement and fulfilment.

The link between goal pursuit and performance has been more securely established in the non-education sector and therefore provides further direction for what determines effectiveness. Most important is the level of challenge of goals.

Specifics of the links between challenging, 'high', goals and performance are reported in Chapter 4 in the section on 'lift' with goals, but more generally, in the non-education sector Locke and Latham (2013) report that conditions of goal acceptance and commitment, goal specificity (more specific goals affect performance more), goal difficulty, and feedback are important in successful goal achievement. The 'acceptance and commitment' feature builds on the earlier work of Erez, Earley, and Hulin (1985) who suggested an individual's participation in setting their own goals resulted in a higher rate of acceptance because they had some self-control over the goal setting process.

In this general sector literature, Locke and Latham (2013) also state that goal setting increases interest and reduces boredom with routine tasks. Increased interest is associated with increased performance. These authors offer that without the necessary resources, a goal (regardless of whether personal or organizational) is unlikely to be attained—a point highlighted in the FAR Model. This resourcing feature also overlaps with the suggestion from IEL in the education sector that resources need to be provided for goal pursuit with the nomination of this as a factor linked to achievement. Locke and Latham (2013) raise that making goals public, i.e. sharing them with others, also impacts on achievement of goals. The public sharing factor linked to achievement emerges later in this book when discussing application of the FAR Model elements.

SMART is a very commonly adopted acronym for describing what is important in goal pursuit both in the education and non-education sectors. SMART stands for Specific, Measurable, Achievable, Realistic and Timely. I find this somewhat unspecific acronym to be useful as a reminder, or overview summary, in goal pursuit but it is often adopted without understanding of the complexity of this topic. For this reason, I am mentioning it here but note that subsequent sections of this book move beyond use of such an overview.

> Think about goal pursuit you have been involved in and respond to the following questions.
>
> ▸ In what ways has goal pursuit you have been involved in led to a sense of achievement and fulfilment?
>
> ▸ If that is the case, how have any goals you have pursued provided you with meaning in life, a target and the associated deep sense of satisfaction referred to by Vorhauser-Smith (2011), or raised your self-efficacy (Leithwood, Aitken, & Jantzi, 2006)?
>
> ▸ To what degree was 'self-concordance' (Sheldon, 2002) evident in such goal pursuit i.e. you selected a goal which was meaningful and linked to your individual values?

Latterly, my deepening interest in the purpose and importance of goal pursuit has led the biologist in me to explore how the body, particularly the brain, actually responds in goal pursuit. It is the area of neuroscience which has provided some evidence of physiological response in goal pursuit and this evidence has been further interpreted by the neuroleadership field.

Links to recent research from neuroscience and neuroleadership

Lafferty and Alford (2010) describe that 'neuroscience' research is being used in the 'neuroleadership' field to look inside the brain to analyse what might affect leadership and management practices. In neuroscience, MRI (Magnetic Resonance Imaging) and EEG (Electroencephalogram) technology have provided the breakthrough in looking at brain functioning because these techniques are purported to map real time reaction to real stimuli. Both the neuroscience and neuroleadership fields are huge (see Ringleb & Rock, 2013) but for my interest area and the purposes of this book, I want to narrow down the fields down to just goal pursuit.

Let me begin with a focus on how neuroleadership authors have interpreted the neuroscience findings on goal pursuit. I need to preface this discussion by also noting that I am in fact interpreting their interpretations! With any such double interpretation, there is always a likelihood of misinterpretation or extrapolation, but I am making every attempt here to reduce the latter. I will begin by reviewing which areas of the brain are currently seen to respond in goal pursuit, followed by the impact of stress on the executive functions in the PFC, conditions which encourage 'approach' as summarized in two popular models, another view on this neuroscience and neuroleadership material linked to goals from Vorhauser-Smith, and my own cautionary note.

Indications of areas of the brain responding in goal pursuit

Multiple areas of the brain are involved in goal pursuit but whilst we have many techniques now for examining brain functioning and we need to be mindful that each has its limitations (Mobbs & McFarland, 2013), there are some indications of where brain activity is relevant.

The hippocampus (linked to attention, memory, emotion, and part of the limbic system) and the amygdala (responsive to threat, functions associated with memory and emotion and social cognition, and also part of the limbic system) are considered to be important in goal pursuit. However, the most significant area associated with goal pursuit and focusing is the prefrontal cortex, PFC, shown with functions in Figure 2.1. The PFC also includes the ventral lateral prefrontal cortex, VLPC, which has a control and inhibiting function.

The biology of the brain is important here, but do not get overwhelmed by this specificity if the brain anatomy is too technical. Just remember that the PFC region is important in goal pursuit! Ochsner, Bunge, Gross and Gabrieli (2002) summarize the research confirming this. They suggest one or more active locations of stimulation in the brain for goal pursuit and state that "...prefrontal regions enable one

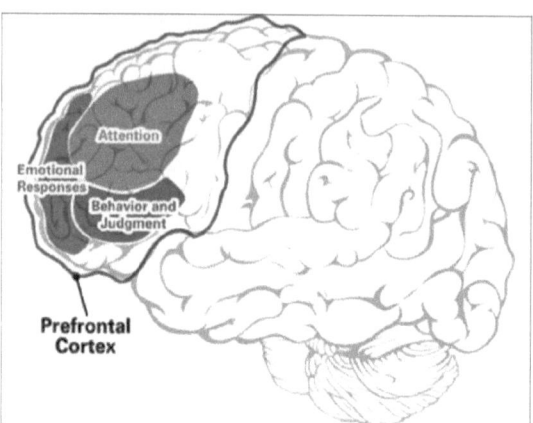

FIGURE 2.1 *Prefrontal region of the brain*

to selectively attend to and maintain goal-relevant information in the mind and resist interference" (p. 1215). It is this part of the brain which 'mediates' *executive functions* linked to organizing and structuring information, planning, monitoring and inhibiting behaviour, making choices and decision making. As Rock, Siegel, Poelmans, and Payne (2012) note, "A lack of stimulation (boredom) and overstimulation (stress) leads to impairment of executive functions, distraction, and lack of focus" (p. 55). I will now explore this 'stress' element a little further.

Stress impact on the executive functions in the PFC

As previously noted, the 'reflective' PFC area of the brain is important for what are often described as the executive functions of the brain such as decision making and goal pursuit. As Rock et al. (2012) also summarize, stress impacts on this functioning—both low and high stress.

It is suggested that when in *low stress* and focused on goal pursuit tasks, the PFC lights up in MRI showing this as the area where brain activity is concentrated. In low stress, positive emotion, and reward conditions, therefore, the PFC is active, responsive and focused in goal pursuit activity. Such a low stressed situation is often linked to what is described as an *approach* (toward, reward) condition in neuroleadership (Rock, 2008) where increased clarity in solving problems, holding focus, is evident. This is summarized in Figure 2.2. It is worthy of note also that the brain responds best to a single focus—a particular point which ties in well with a comment I make later in the book about 'doing few things and doing them well' in goal pursuit.

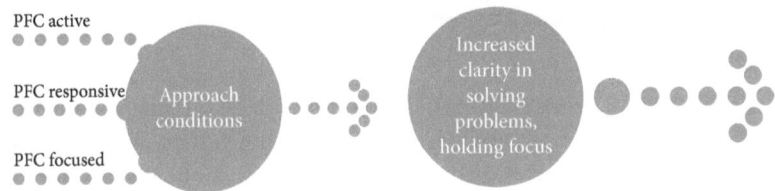

FIGURE 2.2 *Low stress, positive emotion, and reward conditions*

With increasing or *high stress* and negative emotion or punishment conditions, however, activity shifts away from the PFC, catecholamines (stress hormones) flood the brain, oxygen reduces, and less glucose is available to the brain. In these conditions, the reflective PFC part of the brain is seen to somewhat 'turn off' and the reflexive (nonconscious, automatic, and reactive) part of the brain switches on. Such 'turning off' usually results in impaired executive functions in the PFC with subsequent disorganized and unfocused activity dominating. This situation is often described in neuroleadership as an *avoid* (away, threat) response in goal pursuit.

I am going to pause for a little reflection now before moving more deeply into interpretations of this material. When I first engaged with this material on brain regions, *approach* and *avoid conditions*, I felt quite overwhelmed by this thinking. I needed to link this back to my own experience. I invite you to do the same, perhaps guided by the following reflective questions.

> Think about a student you have worked with who has found some specific aspect of their learning very stressful and difficult (if you are a leader, you might consider this from the perspective of one of your staff who is very stressed by goal pursuit).
>
> ▸ What would have been happening to their brain executive functions in this stressful situation?
>
> ▸ Which part of the brain was 'turned off'?
>
> ▸ What could happen in the brain if their stress was reduced?

Conditions which encourage approach

In my initial reading of much of this neuroleadership material, I found the explanations of approach and avoid conditions to be fascinating, mainly because I could see that knowing about such conditions might help me to encourage certain techniques for practical application. This led me to dig more deeply into the neuroleadership literature to explore the exact conditions enabling *approach* to maximize goal pursuit activity.

I am simplifying summaries from Street (2010), Berkman and Rock (2012), Rock and Ringleb (2013) here, but I encourage you to read Berkman and Rock's work for complexity if you thirst for that. In neuroleadership there is a tendency to use acronyms to group ideas associated with such conditions. Two such commonly referred to acronyms are SCARF (status, certainty, autonomy, relatedness, fairness) and AIM (antecedents, integration, maintenance).

The Berkman and Rock (2012) SCARF acronym is used as a summary of the social factors (domains) creating *approach* conditions; in other words, factors maximizing rewards and minimizing threats. You might also want to look at an update in Rock and Cox (2013), particularly on the inter-relatedness between the domains of 'status' and 'relatedness', and 'certainty' and 'relatedness'. My own following interpretation to this SCARF material is an attempt to contextualize the social factors (domains) for goal pursuit:

▶ Status

When individuals perceive a reduction in status (their relative importance in a hierarchy) they are experiencing a component of social pain. The brain is affected in the same way as it would with physical pain (Eisenberger, Lieberman, & Williams, 2003), i.e. the reflective brain functioning is reduced. However status can be enhanced "... when people feel they are learning and improving and when attention is paid to this improvement" (Rock, 2008: 47), and when they are given positive feedback. In these conditions the reflective brain functioning is increased. I interpret from this that goal pursuit and its outcomes should be accorded status and merit if pursuers are to be focused and achieve their goals. It implies that the goals should create learning and improvement, and ongoing positive feedback should be provided throughout the goal pursuit. Key people also need to be given voice and to be involved in goal pursuit rather than have goals imposed upon them.

▶ Certainty

The brain is a pattern-seeking device constantly seeking outcomes to satisfy its craving for certainty so that prediction and meeting expectations can occur. This creates a reward response with increased dopamine levels in the brain (Schultz, 1999). The PFC is less fatigued when there is greater certainty. In essence, goal pursuit as an activity in itself can be seen as pattern seeking because in approaches such as the FAR Model, clear planning and incremental progression through detailed, explicit, improvement steps is part of the process, as is clarity around expectations of achievement. Within goal pursuit therefore clarification of gain-framed actions and outcomes contributes to certainty.

▶ Autonomy

The brain prefers choices as well as some control (agency) over the environment and choices. This places individuals in the driver's seat which, in turn, results in a reward, *approach*, response. Being tightly monitored, however, leads to a sense of poor control of process and outcomes and creates an *avoid* response. In goal pursuit, therefore, those affected by goals should both be involved in their selection (having choice) and have a considerable degree of self-directedness in the way they are pursued (having control).

▶ Relatedness

Mobbs and McFarland (2013) suggest, "... affiliation activates the brain's reward network" (p. 499). The brain responds well to individuals having a sense of belonging, and we feel safe in belonging (Cacioppo & Patrick, 2008). Such belonging is enhanced when we are included rather than excluded, work collaboratively and supportively with others, and share ideas etc. I interpret from this that sharing, critiquing, and working collaboratively with others who create a response of safety and trust is therefore important in goal pursuit. The material in Chapter 4 on lowering defensiveness and enhancing dialogue in authentic collaboration as an underpinning to the FAR Model provides direction for enhancing this relatedness element because it encourages buddy systems, mentoring, and coaching in goal pursuit.

▶ Fairness

An individual's threat and avoidance response is easily triggered by a sense of unfairness. Increasing transparency, communication, involvement, establishing clear expectations, process outlines and allowing people to establish those expectations (Rock, 2008) can enhance a sense of fairness. My interpretation here is that those supporting, appraising, assessing or reviewing goals should always strive to create bilateral (two-sided input), objective (evidence-based discussion), mutual decision making interactions associated with the expectations and process for goal pursuit. Once again, the sort of non-defensive, dialogue-based interactions that lead to bilateral decision-making elaborated in my previous work (Piggot-Irvine, 2012) and in Chapter 4 of this book contributes to the element of fairness.

Figure 2.3 provides a summary of the conditions creating *approach* response that are linked to goal pursuit.

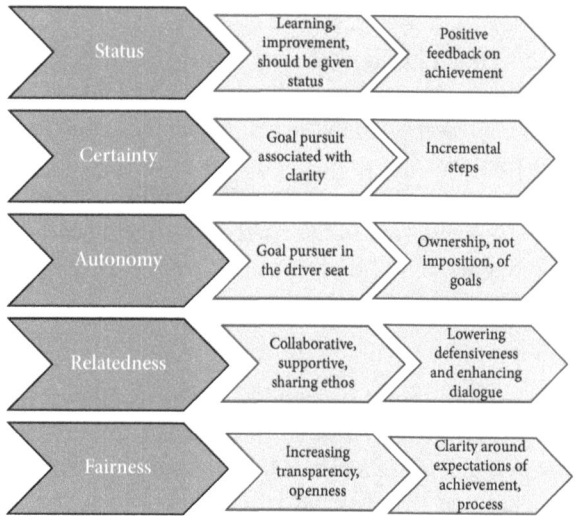

FIGURE 2.3   *Conditions creating approach response in goal pursuit*

Berkman and Rock (2012) further outline a more specific acronym, AIM, as a model covering three critical components in goal pursuit i.e. antecedents, integration, and managing rewards and anticipation. The model is purported to be based on research from the SMART model, Goal Systems Theory, and Cybernetic models. The AIM model involves:

* **Antecedents**
   * *Stickiness* (engaging parts of our brain which help ideas and behaviours stick, become memorable. Linking goals to specific triggers and making them easy to think about is important);

- *Motivation* (setting gain-framed, positively focused goals helps to achieve longer-term, more sustainable results. Knowing what you are motivated by helps in setting gain-framed goals); and
- *Social context* (the brain craves group context and connection in goal pursuit—this and 'motivation' overlap with the SCARF element of relatedness. I have heard neuroleadership experts suggest that this is the most important of the components).

* **Integration** (ongoing goal pursuit)—knowing and articulating 'why' you are setting a goal and 'how' you will achieve it (and shifting gears between why and how), including implementation intentions and knowledge of obstacles and ways to overcome those, is essential.
* **Maintenance**—managing rewards and anticipation (turning goals into habits)—the brain loves to anticipate and 'predict' receiving rewards. Habits are formed through small victories which create resulting rewards. Repeatedly practising activity associated with a goal leads to habits and eventually the habit becomes independent of the reward and is automatic.

In this AIM model there are elements giving us direction for some of the technical, process features in goal pursuit. The 'maintenance' and 'social context' elements in particular, however, further emphasize the interpersonal component which overlaps with some features of the SCARF acronym. This is strengthened by an emphasis in the work of Uhl-Bein and Marion (2009) who state that people:

> ...must compromise and cooperate in order to achieve their personal goals. In this process, people share ideas and knowledge, different bits of knowledge and ideas merge, diverge, and elaborate. The net outcome is learning, adaptability, innovation, and new order (p. 641).

This collaborative component, as noted in Chapter 1, is one of the key principles underpinning the FAR Model offered for goal pursuit in this book. The compromise, co-operation, sharing suggestions from Uhl-Bein and Marion are embedded in such collaboration.

> Return to your thinking about the student you have worked with who has found some specific aspect of their learning very stressful and difficult (if you are a leader, you might consider this from the perspective of one of your staff who is very stressed by goal pursuit).

> Describe the conditions that would need to be in place for this student to have their brain working in the *approach* response?

> What implications do those conditions have for the way that you would be creating a supportive teaching and learning environment?

Another view on this neuroscience and neuroleadership material linked to goals

Vorhauser-Smith (2011), I believe, nicely summarizes much of this neuroscience and neuroleadership material linked to goals. She notes that the setting of goals channels attention. In its default state, she says, the brain is noisy with dozens of thoughts, but focusing our attention on anything redirects random neural firing patterns to focused pathways. Once we consciously focus on a goal, the brain subconsciously evaluates goal-relevant information consistent with achieving the goal. Like radar, it selectively notices incoming data influencing the goal whilst inhibiting irrelevant information to prevent overload. She also states that goals motivate work performance and findings show that though we gain satisfaction from reviewing completed goals, we are *more motivated* by what still needs to be done. She concludes by saying, "Achieving a goal is fulfilling, while focusing on a goal to pursue is energizing" (p. 6).

My cautionary note

The discussion I have offered so far might suggest my fascination with the neuroleadership material has led me to some conclusive recommendations on application in the goal pursuit context. It is at this point that I need to insert a cautionary note in terms of the progress in my thinking. Latterly I have been digging much more deeply into the neuroscience 'foundations' purported to support neuroleadership conclusions. In this 'dig' I have painfully tried to decipher neuroscience articles on decision making and goal pursuit (Louie & Glimcher, 2012, as just one example). I have also connected with neuroscientists like the wonderful, and sadly recently deceased, Joan King, to try to clarify understanding. In an attempt to seek a balanced view, I have read articles such as Gordon's (2013) deconstruction of the arguments for and against neuroleadership and also attended neuroleadership workshops.

My current thinking on the neuroleadership material is at what I recently described as the 'amber' (orange and 'slow down') light phase. Almost every neuroscience article I have read fails to show indication of clarity around brain functioning sufficient to reveal all of what appear to be categorical conclusions drawn in some of the neuroleadership material. In support of this, Louie and Glimcher (2012) assert that the brain "... mechanism underlying comparative evaluation in decision making is unknown" (p. 16). Decision making is strongly involved in goal pursuit so if this mechanism is unknown, I have pondered how many other assertions in some of the neuroleadership writing about goal pursuit can be totally credible. Miller, as early as 2008, was alerting us to this concern in more general about neuroleadership assertions. He said: "People seem to believe that images of brain activity make a behavioral observation more real, says bioethicist Éric Racine of the Institut de Recherches Cliniques de Montréal in Canada. Racine calls this effect "neurorealism" and says it's often amplified by media coverage that oversimplifies research findings and glosses over caveats" (p. 1413). In summary, I am currently weighing up the degree to which the neuroleadership literature is oversimplifying the neuroscience findings!

However, despite my cautionary tale here about the validity claims of neuroleadership on goal pursuit, many facets of the SCARF and AIM material resonate strongly with both what other researchers who do not look into the brain (non-neuroscientists) have reported upon and my own practical experience in working on goal pursuit with hundreds of individuals. Regardless of the strength of the neuroscience underpinnings for neuroleadership, this experience puts me in a position of almost total agreement with the SCARF and AIM statements around what creates effective goal pursuit. It is from this position that I offer ideas for goal pursuit in the following sections of this book. In the next chapter, for example, I will draw on my own experience in elaborating the FAR Model for goal pursuit.

> ... My current thinking on the neuroleadership material is at what I recently described as the "amber" (orange and "slow down") light phase.

Summary

- Goals are important for attaining direction, purpose and meaning.
- Research shows clear links between goal pursuit and motivation, focus, achievement and fulfilment.
- Goals must be personally compelling, challenging and achievable.
- 'Engagement' is often seen to occur when students make an investment in their learning and take pride in accomplishing learning objectives, yet goal pursuit has yet to become real and compelling in schools.
- Evidence-based, informed, goal pursuit is important, as indicated in the FAR Model.
- Self-concordance, matching personal values in goal pursuit, is important in enhancing commitment.
- The most significant area of the brain associated with goal pursuit and focusing is the prefrontal cortex (PFC).
- Minimizing threat and stress maximizes *approach* conditions in the PFC which enhances goal pursuit.
- We gain satisfaction from reviewing completed goals, we are *more motivated* by what still needs to be done.

3
A Simple, Yet Detailed, Model for Goal Pursuit

Abstract: *In Chapter 3, the FAR model is described in detail. The chapter begins with discussion of AR as the core of the model. The 'action' and 'research' dual purposes are described as well as opinion on the relevancy of this approach. Each of the Preparatory, Reconnaissance, Implementation, Evaluation, Recommendations and Reporting phases of the Model are then outlined alongside examples of implementation in schools and the wider education context. Multiple cycles of these phases are noted as likely and collaborative and reflection are essential at every phase of the FAR Model for ensuring ownership and sustained improvements. The key underpinnings of the model are described, drawing upon my 20-year obsession with an AR orientation (Piggot-Irvine, 2012; Piggot-Irvine & Bartlett, 2008; Piggot-Irvine, 2009; Piggot-Irvine, Connelly, Curry, Hanna, Moodie, Palmer, Peri, & Thompson, 2011). A distinctive section of this chapter is associated with discussion of Goal Attainment Scaling (GAS) as a tool for self, peer, or group dialogue as evaluation in goal pursuit. This tool is virtually unknown outside the counselling, care, and psychology sectors yet it has been exceptionally well received when I have introduced it within the education sector.*

Keywords: Action research; Goal Attainment Scaling; Preparatory, Reconnaissance, Implementation, Evaluation, Recommendations and Reporting phases

Piggot-Irvine, Eileen. *Goal Pursuit in Education Using Focused Action Research.* New York: Palgrave Macmillan, 2015. DOI: 10.1057/9781137505125.0008.

Introduction

This chapter provides an outline of the FAR Model and each of its phases for goal pursuit beginning with background to AR itself. Where appropriate I use examples in each of the phased activities in the model to demonstrate application. Overall, as you read this chapter, keep in mind that the Model focuses on few things being done well!

Background to AR as the core of the FAR model for goal pursuit

The FAR model, as the name suggests, is based on an AR approach. AR is a relatively popular developmental research methodology which has both data collection ('research') and change ('action') elements (Piggot-Irvine et al., 2011). The FAR model, though not 'research' as it is normally thought of in some areas of academia, does emphasize the objective collection and use of data in decision making. AR itself has a cyclical orientation (iterative planning, acting, reflecting and evaluating). It is highly developmental and practical in its intent and it is the latter, combined with all of the other elements noted, that makes it suitable as an approach to goal pursuit. Zuber-Skerritt (2012) adds that AR is also democratic, participative, and collaborative: elements that align with the authentic collaboration principle I have already noted as an underpinning to the FAR Model.

Action researchers often espouse, or articulate, claims of personal, team, organizational, and community (and less frequently global) improvement, sustained change, and transformation, as shown by a wide range of supporters including Coghlan and Brannick (2010), Cardno (2003), Stringer (2007), and Wadsworth (2011) to name but a few. Several action researchers also proclaim outcomes of empowerment or emancipation (e.g., McTaggart, 1991; Reason & Bradbury, 2001; Stringer, 2007). Such emancipatory ideals are not so strongly the intent of the FAR Model but certainly the improvement/transformation outcome is anticipated and links to the overall developmental purpose of AR.

There is always a degree of flexibility and open-endedness in AR. Coghlan and Brannick (2010) support this in stating, "AR has a large degree of messiness and unpredictability about it, in that it is research in real-life action" (p. 69). AR, therefore, does not always occur in a linear, hierarchical, and predictable way. Stringer (2007) extends this by suggesting it is also ongoing when stating, "... a good AR project often has no well-defined ending" (p. 164).

AR is contextually specific and therefore the outcomes from it are usually considered to be non-generalizable. Here, generalizable means the outcomes of AR are not usually considered to be transferable to a different context. They are, however, often stimulants for similar approaches in other contexts.

AR that lacks informed or evidence/data-based decision making is often seen as "sloppy research" (Dick, 2004, p. 16), a "... messy and weak form of research because it has been practised without appropriate rigour" (Cardno, 2003, p. vii). Such sloppiness can threaten the reputation of the approach and some decades ago led Winter (1987) to conclude that it was frequently "... dismissed as muddled science" (p. 2). When such 'sloppy' AR research has been practised, it has resulted in writers such as Brooker and Macpherson (1999) noting that the reporting of AR has sometimes been little more than picturesque journeys of self-indulgent descriptions. Such sloppiness is not a feature of the FAR Model employment in goal pursuit, or many other AR approaches that are conducted by credible colleagues in this field.

The FAR Model is an example of AR which *does* involve informed decision making. The collection of data/evidence is given high priority. Rigour is extended also when the exploration of theory and previous research as part of being 'informed' precedes implementation of action.

Detailed depth in planning alongside a strong emphasis on engaging and authentically collaborating with others is designed to further enhance rigour in AR generally, and especially the FAR Model. This is especially clear when the trustworthiness of the findings is critiqued in feedback by colleagues. Rigour is further enhanced when findings are publicly reported, even if that reporting is to those in a hierarchical position or colleagues within the organization.

The FAR model

As you read this section I would like you refer back to Figure 1.1, the FAR Model. I will now explain the FAR Model more elaborately. Though the Model is shown as somewhat sequential, in fact it incorporates activities that frequently overlap and there is iterative, or cyclical, movement between the elements. I have not always found that there is a linear sequence to activity in goal pursuit and the Model reflects a similar pattern. Just as an example of this, often I have experienced that the evaluation of goal achievement occurs incrementally in several places and phases in the Model rather than as an end of goal pursuit activity. Each of the phases of the FAR Model is elaborated in the following sections.

Preparation

A first Preparatory phase activity in the FAR Model involves all key stakeholders (those influencing and those impacted) in clarifying what the underpinning principles—both leadership and implementation principles—will be for the goal pursuit. In Chapter 4, my own thoughts on the underpinnings of shift in depth, lift in challenge, and authentic collaboration will be outlined in detail. I consider these to be generic underpinning principles; however there will inevitably be further principles that are relevant to specific organizations that need to be added by context specific stakeholders. Regardless of what the additional underpinning principles might be, this initial clarifying activity is as important, if not more important, than just about any other in the Model. I encourage those I have worked with in employing the FAR Model to distil their ideas about the underpinning principles into almost a 'protocol' to guide every other phase of activity. Chapter 6 includes an example of a template for distilling the underpinning principles.

Priority setting by the governing body and senior leadership of an organization, selection of goals to match priorities, and allocation of resources to those goals are the three next Preparatory phase activities most commonly associated with goal preparation for goal pursuit in the FAR Model. Frequently the governing body or leadership group set priorities for a term of time, whether that is a year or multiple years. Often these priorities are influenced by national or regional direction. In turn, the organization usually sets specific, strategic (overarching, guiding) goals aligning with those higher level priorities. If alignment of goals is to occur in an organization, then those strategic organization level goals should significantly influence the focus for subsequent team and individual goals. My own experience with organizations has shown over and over how important such alignment is and this is confirmed by Mobbs and McFarland (2013) who state: "... job goals and aspirations should be clear between the individual and the organization" (p. 504). I use the term 'cascading' to describe the way in which higher level priorities should then fold-out into specific goals at an organization, team or individual level in an organization, as shown in Figure 3.1.

As I have noted earlier in Chapter 2, various authors highlight the importance of cascading and alignment. You might recall the report from Kaplan and Norton (2001) that only approximately seven percent of employees understand what is expected of them to achieve goals in the non-education sector. It is evident therefore that cascading and alignment has not occurred at an intensive, full engagement of staff, level in most organizations outside education. Yet such alignment is crucial if the ultimate outcome of goal pursuit is to be improved performance of individuals, teams and the organization—and especially important in education if improved learning is part of goal pursuit.

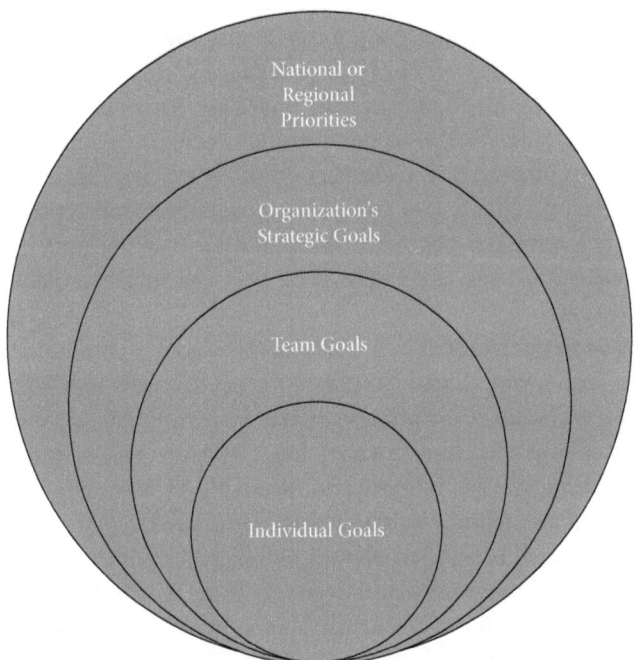

FIGURE 3.1   *Cascading of goals*

In my experience, improved performance occurs most significantly when goals are genuinely shared and aligned: when those impacted by the goal feel they have a voice in creating and helping pursue the goal. Such sharing builds relationships when people see themselves as part of the task, and enhanced relationships, in turn, build trust. There is a direct link here with Berkman and Rock's (2012) neuroleadership SCARF model elements of both creating 'status' and 'fairness' as social conditions, and also the AIM model 'social context' element.

In my experience improved performance occurs most significantly when goals are genuinely shared and aligned: when those impacted by the goal feel they have a voice in creating and helping pursue the goal.

Though not an excuse for poor cascading and shared goals, Uhl-Bein and Marion (2009) remind us that cascading is complex and difficult because of dynamics involved in the early stage alignment of individual goals with the leader's vision of a goal in goal pursuit. They point out that a shared need instead usually starts for employees with a 'what's in it for me?' question. They contend "...if interdependence is not inherent or acknowledged, the likelihood of fully engaging others is slim" (p. 642). Sheldon (2002) adds weight to this argument when stressing the importance of 'self-concordance' (selecting goals which are meaningful and link to personal values), and notes: "Because if non-self-representative goals do not have the person's full emotional backing and volitional support, such goals are not-likely to be well-energized, protected, and attained" (p. 73).

Locke and Latham (2002) offer that the way a goal is presented by leaders is also important. Clearly explained goals increase motivation, but where little explanation occurs, motivation lowers. In gaining ownership in goal cascading therefore, a leader has a considerable task (when do they not you might ask!) in ensuring ownership through alignment and cascading if goals are to be whole-heartedly pursued.

In summary, goals selected should be linked in some way to higher level priorities if alignment and focus in direction is to occur in an organization. The creation of those goals should also be a shared process if engagement is to result.

An example might help here. A Board of Governors in a school I recently consulted with chose as a goal to 'focus learning' for all students in a way that created stronger links between the school and caregivers/parents. This goal aligned to two priorities in a regional plan for education:

1. To strengthen student learning via enhanced focus on specific, individualized, improvement goals; and
2. To enhance school-caregiver/parent interaction in improving student learning.

In this example, cascading occurred at all levels shown in Figure 3.1. The regional priorities were aligned to organizational, team and student level goals. The school leader (Principal A) and every team leader and teacher in School A cascaded and specified the alignment even further by creating their own performance review key leadership goal as: 'To establish focused learning goals for every student and to do this in a way that enhanced the school-caregiver interaction'. Additionally, every student was guided to set a focused, individualized, improvement goal to enhance one area of learning during the term.

Another example will illustrate such cascading in the non-education sector. In a regional government education office I consulted with, the Chief Executive Officer (CEO) chose an organization-wide goal as: 'To implement standardized communication processes between each of the five offices located in the region'. This goal linked directly to a national office directive to ensure the existence of clear and concise, standardized communication systems throughout the country. In turn, each leader in the regional offices had as a personal performance review goal for the year: 'To collaborate with other regional leaders to set up a system for standardized clear and concise communications systems'. Alignment and cascading was evident throughout the whole organization.

The discussion about alignment brings us to an important point when discussing cascading of goals: a point noted in Chapter 1 of the importance of critical connection between performance review goal pursuit and general goal alignment incorporating cascading. I am often stunned when leaders in organizations imply that performance review goal setting is an *additional* activity to goal pursuit. I have frequently observed two sets of goals established—those that are organizational and those for performance review. When I have seen this, one of my first tasks as a consultant has been to assist the organization to align performance review with all other goal pursuit.

It's time to pause again to allow you time to personally reflect on the activity described so far in the Preparation Phase of the FAR Model.

> Consider your previous experiences with goal pursuit.
>
> ▸ To what extent was there dialogue about underpinning principles that would guide the goal pursuit?
>
> ▸ If dialogue did occur, what sort of principles emerged and were these upheld in the subsequent process of goal pursuit?
>
> ▸ Similarly, describe the extent to which there was dialogue about, and commitment to ensuring, alignment and cascading of organizational, team, and personal goals, and also alignment to performance review goals.
>
> ▸ If dialogue did occur and alignment was established, what evidence was there of impact of that alignment?

A further important point linked to the Preparatory phase of goal pursuit is associated with how the goal is framed. An overly optimistic framing of the goal is not something I encourage. I know there is a considerable voice of support for expressing goals, or any other issues in organizations, only in 'appreciative' or 'ideal' terms (Ospina, Dodge, Godsoe, Minieri, Salvador & Schall, 2002) and I have a degree of support for taking a positive rather than negative stance. However, there are many situations, when naming and tackling a problem is required rather than engagement in what can amount to highly avoiding activity if only positive activities and outcomes are in focus. The FAR Model does not support the introduction of goal pursuit as activity only looking vaguely at the 'ideal' or possible solutions but rather it is strongly prefaced by a rigorous consideration of all aspects, good and not-so-good, associated with the goal. Such thinking is in keeping with that recently shared by Joanna Swann (2013), a former colleague. She summarizes, "... it is important to focus initially on the problem context and the formulation of one or more pressing and/or significant problems" (p. 45).

Following the selection of goals to cascade from higher level priorities, a next Preparatory phase activity in goal pursuit shown in the FAR Model is the alignment of resources to ensure goal achievement. The very best goal pursuit approaches I have seen in organizations have been those that were well resourced in terms of leadership guidance and direction setting, financial support (particularly in time release) for goal pursuit, and mentoring or professional development if required.

For example, Principal A set up extensive professional development to engage teachers in learning about helping students to focus in learning and allocated funding for time release for the development, provided meeting expenses for caregiver interactions, and personally mentored staff in their work on this with students. Similarly the CEO in the government education office, though placing less emphasis on professional development of all staff, worked with team leaders to create an understanding of what standardized communication would involve and then provided time and refreshments for multiple team meetings designed to ensure the team leaders rolled-out the communication processes.

Preparatory activities are therefore critical to the success of goal pursuit. Priority setting by Governors and leaders, selection of goals to match priorities (including linking performance review and other goal setting) and aligning and cascading goals, as well as the allocation of resources to pursue goals, are all key activities. Once these priorities are established it is possible to move into the next phase of the FAR Model where the current situation associated with a goal is thoroughly examined.

> *Preparatory activities are therefore critical ... priority setting, selection of goals to match priorities (including linking performance review)... aligning and cascading goals... allocation of resources.*

Reconnaissance: current situation analysis

The FAR model emphasises a *Reconnaissance* phase which involves identification of the exact nature of the current situation associated with the selected goal as well as a review of current thinking/theory about the topic of focus. Swann (2013) supports such a current situation analysis in stating, "... the context should be scrutinized before launching a solution" (p. 46).

The Reconnaissance phase begins with rigorous data/evidence collection in terms of current practices (and gaps) associated with the goal. I have long and consistently expressed (Cardno & Piggot-Irvine, 1996; Piggot-Irvine, 2009) that decisions in any AR-oriented activity, of which the FAR Model for goal pursuit is an example, should be based on evidence. Such evidence provides rigour to decision making about recommended improvements. The emphasis on rigour, I confess, is not always so widely shown in AR generally and as I have noted in an earlier book (Piggot-Irvine, 2009) "... I would venture to suggest that there is a degree of derision associated with the mention of "data" for some action researchers. However, like Busher and Harris (2000), I believe that evidence-based research should be used as the foundation for improvement" (p. 5).

Multiple sources of data can be collected as part of the current situation analysis in the FAR Model: data from diverse groups, contexts, as well as differing types of data. Such multiple perspective orientation to the data collection is frequently described as 'triangulating' or 'cross-checking' of data (Cohen, Manion & Morrison, 2007). Most of the data will be qualitative (or in words) but I also encourage quantitative (numeric and able to be statistically analysed) data collection or even a combination of both in what is called a mixed method approach (Creswell & Plano Clark, 2011; Johnson & Onwuegbuzie, 2004).

A raft of methods for collecting data can also be used in the FAR Model in the Reconnaissance phase. For example, interviews, questionnaires, focus groups, and observation are probably the most typically used methods, as well as analysing existing documents and records. If you want further detail on any of these methods, or others that are less mainstream such as repertory grid technique, or nominal group, several are outlined in terms of definition, purpose, explanation, and application in Piggot-Irvine and Bartlett (2008). Table 3.1 provides an overview of selected data collection methods that could be used in the FAR Model.

TABLE 3.1 *Selected data collection methods*

Observation	Interview
Nominal group	Focus group
Learning circle	Survey
Photo voice	World café
Repertory grid	Documentary analysis

Returning to the two example sector cases already noted for the Preparatory phase of the FAR Model, each individual leader of the goal pursuit used varied, triangulated, methods to examine the current situation in the Reconnaissance phase. Principal A and her senior leadership team collected feedback in surveys from students, teachers, and parents/caregivers on their perceptions of focus both in student learning *and* parent/caregiver involvement in this focusing. In collaboration with the teachers, she also examined student work (documentary analysis), as well as teacher performance goals, to determine the type and quality of goals that were set. The CEO and his leadership team in the government sector education organization conducted interviews with staff to gain feedback on the current state of communication systems, reviewed all documentation available on those systems and they met frequently to share ideas in the analysis of this material.

Following rigorous data collection, the next activity in the Reconnaissance phase involves information gathering (literature, research etc.) from beyond the organization on what is seen to be effective practice associated with the topic of the goal. Put another way, it involves becoming 'informed' through some thinking and theory on the topic. Why do this, you might ask? Essentially, in my opinion, the answer to this is that without looking at some previous thinking, theory, and research we run the risk of ignorantly or blindly implementing change with a consequence of wasted resources and misdirected action. Thinking, theory, and previous research on what works well can influence the success of practice. It helps to avoid the issue which Sagor (2000) suggests occurs, "... when actions are taken in accordance with an incorrect or inadequate theory, the underlying problem continues to fester" (p. 61).

However, looking at previous thinking, theory and research are not always a welcomed activity for those outside academic organizations. I have previously described that theory and research:

> ...are often seen as being remote from day-to-day work by practitioners... I believe there are three reasons for this:
> - Busy practitioners have little time to extensively explore theory and research
> - The densely theoretical reporting of much research is often seen as being 'impenetrable' or unreadable
> - Practitioners have often had little assistance to develop literature search skills. (Piggot-Irvine, 2009: 6).

Because conducting what amounts to a 'literature review' is such a foreign activity to most practitioners, I usually begin this activity in the Reconnaissance phase of the FAR Model by actively supporting the development of skills to help participants to know how to source and then select a few readable and useful key articles. I also show them how to quickly distil the key points from an article that are pertinent to their goal, to record their summaries, and mostly importantly guide them in how to work collaboratively to quickly share this task through delegation.

> Consider your previous experiences with goal pursuit.
>
> ▸ How did you collect data on the current situation before making changes/improvements?
>
> ▸ What previous literature or theory did you refer to in order to become 'informed' about other studies, and what thinking, or research had been conducted on your chosen goal topic?
>
> ▸ If you conducted such evidence-based analysis before embarking on change/improvement with your goal, how do you think such analysis influenced your thinking about changes?

After you've collected data on the current situation, as well as becoming informed about previous thinking, theory and research on effective practice, you need to draw conclusions about where improvement is needed associated with your chosen goal. Again, collaboration is critical in this highly reflective task. Engagement and buy-in by those who will be implementing the improvements is, in my experience, a vital activity in the FAR Model. Many authors urge that any organizational change begins with the active participation of key individuals in shared decision making about the change goals (Appelbaum & Wohl, 2000; Bushe & Marshak, 2009). Good leaders I have worked with make an extraordinary effort to ensure the key implementers are present in deciding what is to be acted upon but that they are also equal participants in the decision making. The 'relational' element of the neuroleadership SCARF model also places great emphasis on this component of focused thinking. The following chapter outlining the authentic collaboration underpinning of the FAR Model details how such participation occurs in an equally contributing way via processes of dialogue and non-defensive interactions.

> *Following data collection on the current situation ... becoming informed about previous thinking, theory and research on effective practice ... conclusions are then drawn ... collaboration is critical in this highly reflective task.*

Principal A is an example of a good leader who meticulously attended to creating engagement in the 'becoming informed' activity associated with the Reconnaissance phase in the FAR Model. She decided to conduct her own review of multiple publications and research on both the topic of how to focus learning (including information on goal pursuit) and also how to engage teachers in 'buying-in' to any approaches adopted. She did this prior review in order to select a small number of readable, yet informative, articles. She then shared with her leadership team what she thought were the key features in the articles associated with effective practice but she was careful to do this in a way which indicated this was just her own thinking and she was open to new perspectives from the team. The team equally divided up the articles to be reviewed, took a week to conduct the review and then met again to report back on their findings and to summarize the overall implications for their own goal pursuit. Following this review, Principal A and the leadership team facilitated multiple meetings where teachers, caregivers/parents and governors were invited to share in this learning in experiential ways.

Once decisions are made about what is to be actioned or implemented for improvement then a final step of the Reconnaissance phase is detailed planning for the Implementation phase or as it is sometimes called, the 'Intervention' phase. I encourage the planning for improvement steps to include clear timelines and measurable outcomes. As an example plan to demonstrate the sort of detail I am alluding to, I have included a plan that a student in School A completed as an individual improvement plan. The student is some way down the pecking order from Principal A and the CEO whom I have used so far as examples, but the principles of planning are no different and this plan shows how well the adoption of learning cascaded throughout the whole school. The layout and content of the plan for this student is the same as for leaders or anyone else in an organization and therefore I hope the plan illustrates that.

'Sean' (name anonymized), the 11-year-old student who drew up this plan, did so only after he had completed the prior activities detailed so far for the FAR Model. He had selected a goal for his own learning enhancement (you will recall the principal's goal included ensuring every student had a personal goal for learning enhancement). In Sean's case, his learning enhancement involved improving the way he wrote project reports. He collected previous feedback from teachers on report writing and also spoke to them about what they thought he needed to focus on for improvement (his data collection) as well as requesting exemplars of good reports. He conducted a Google search and read several articles about what good report writing involved and determined criteria for effective report writing (he became 'informed', in other words). He decided what he was going to focus on for improvement and wrote the following plan shown in Table 3.2 to summarize both what he had done in the Reconnaissance phase and to plan for his Implementation phase.

TABLE 3.2 *Sean's deep action plan showing Reconnaissance and Implementation phases*

Goal	Actions	Measurable Outcomes	Date for Completion
To improve the way that I write project reports	*Reconnaissance*		
	1. Do some reading, check the internet, ask my teachers about the criteria for effective report writing	1. Knowledge of effective project writing and a clear set of criteria written for this	April 10th
	2. Check/review how I write reports currently by assessing two previous reports against the criteria	2. A summary of findings from 1. is recorded against effectiveness criteria (EC)	May 15th
	3. Ask teacher for exemplars of good reports and use them to check if my criteria are sound	3. Updated EC if required	May 25th
	Planning for Improvement		
	4. Think about the results from 1–3 and develop an outline of the way I will improve report writing, detailing each step	4. Specific steps for improvement developed	June 20th
	Carrying out Improvement		
	5. Put my steps for improvement in place for 2–3 reports. Pay attention to further improving after feedback and assessments are received on each	5. Reports written using criteria and steps for improvement	Mid-August
	6. Keep a diary of my improvement progress	6. Ongoing reflections on progress recorded	September 15

Sean's plan is not a typical one I have observed for improvement. More frequently plans contain just broad, non-specific, statements outlining improvement such as 'to get better assessments for reports'. Sean's approach, like that of others who work with me using the FAR Model, is '*deep*'. Although in the following chapter, I elaborate on what such depth means, I want to note here that I consider depth to be so important I have categorized it as an underpinning element of the FAR Model.

In summary, the Reconnaissance phase in the FAR Model is focused on rigorous, evidence-based decision making on the existing situation associated with a goal, becoming 'informed through reviewing previous thinking and research on elements of effectiveness linked to the goal, and constructing specific steps for improvement and implementation.

> Consider your previous experiences with goal pursuit.
>
> ▸ How would you summarize your experience of engaging in Reconnaissance phase activity as described throughout this section so far?
>
> ▸ How rigorous and evidence-based was decision making on the existing situation associated with the goal?
>
> ▸ How deeply were specific steps for improvement and implementation planned?

Implementation

A goal pursuit *Implementation* phase follows the latter well 'informed' and planned deep goal setting activities in the FAR Model. At this phase the deep plan is carried out.

It is important at this phase of the Model that resource provision continues in order to ensure that any development, time allocation, and support associated with improvement is ongoing. Principal A, for example, made it a key priority to hold regular meetings with teachers, caregivers/parents, and governors to provide full training for all teachers to enable them to have the skills both to introduce focused goal pursuit by students *and* engage parents/caregivers in supporting students in the goal selection and achievement. They continued these meetings during implementation of the planned activities to enable ongoing support. Principal A also provided one-to-one mentoring where required for any teacher.

The CEO in the regional government education office made sure he had created a strong delegation process for team leaders to roll-out the implementation of the standardized communication systems. He also continued to hold weekly meetings to check the quality of implementation with the team leaders as it was being rolled out.

The type of Implementation phase activity both Principal A and the CEO conducted were well described in the deep planning conducted in the previous Reconnaissance phase. Sean's plan in Table 3.2 shows an example of planning ahead with clarity about timelines and specific measurable outcomes. In my experience, if the measurable outcomes in the plan are specific they will provide clear indicators for assessment/evaluation of the achievement of objectives in the next phase of the FAR Model. It is this 'review', evaluation of achievement, phase of the FAR Model that I will discuss next.

At the Implementation phase the deep plan is carried out. It is important at this phase of the Model that resource provision continues in order to ensure that any development, time allocation, and support associated with improvement is ongoing.

Evaluation of achievement of Implementation

Following the goal Implementation phase, an *Evaluation* of achievement of implementation is the next phase in the FAR Model. Evaluation is not a concluding activity because frequently it leads to ideas, indicators and recommendations for further improvement. Evaluation can occur in multiple ways but I have found that well-articulated anticipated, or expected, outcomes stated in the deep goal planning considerably assist with clarifying the approaches to evaluation—and there are many approaches available for use. Essentially the same points raised under the Reconnaissance phase heading, apply equally here i.e. the importance of rigorous, triangulated data, as well as engaging others authentically in data collection.

I return to Principal A to illustrate application of this Evaluation phase. For data collection tools she employed surveys, student/teacher/parent and caregiver interviews and focus groups, documentary analysis of goal plans and specific learning evidence, as well as a trial of a goal attainment scaling system (GAS). This was quite some undertaking and she demonstrated once again a well-informed, evidence/data based approach to the evaluation. Most importantly also, she ensured that the analysis, interpretation and reflection on the findings from this data collection was conducted collaboratively with key people who had been engaged in implementing improvements in the previous phase.

The CEO in the government education office employed considerably fewer data collection tools, but substantially more than the majority of goal pursuers I have observed where a complete absence of data collection to evaluate outcomes and impact has been evident. The CEO held one-to-one interviews with team leaders to gain their feedback at the end of the Implementation phase. He also asked me, as an independent consultant, to conduct a survey with all staff to gather their feedback on the roll-out and its effectiveness. The CEO and I then worked with the team leaders to jointly analyse the data collected and then collectively reflected upon what the findings revealed for further improvement.

In both of these example cases there were areas for further improvement suggested which the Principal and CEO equally enthusiastically saw as opportunities for enhanced quality. In both cases also considerable celebration of achievement occurred as those involved reflected upon the findings.

In the case of Sean, the student in School A, the activities for data collection for his Evaluation phase were a little more humble yet no less significant. As shown in Table 3.3, Sean analysed his improved reports, sought further feedback from his teachers (a type of interview), and also completed a GAS for teacher and self-review. He then reflected upon what further improvement was required.

TABLE 3.3   Sean's Evaluation phase activity

Goal	Actions	Measurable Outcomes	Date for Completion
To improve the way that I write project reports	*Review/Evaluation* 7. Seek feedback from teachers on improvements and use feedback as guide to further enhance both reports and EC	7. Improvement shown as recorded in marks and feedback on reports. Improvement summarized against EC	Dec 15
	8. Complete GAS as self-review and ask teacher to rate my achievement as well	8. Achievement espousals compared with teacher review	Dec 15
	9. Analysis of results reflected upon	9. Further areas for improvement identified	Dec 15
	10. Review EC if required.	10. Refined EC	Dec 15

Consider your previous experiences with goal pursuit.

▸ How would you summarize your experience of engaging in Evaluation phase activity as described throughout this section so far?

▸ If it existed at all, how rigorous was data collection on the effectiveness, outcomes and impacts of the Implementation phase associated with the goal?

▸ Describe the way in which emphasis was paid to collaborative analysis of the data and if that occurred, what the impact of the collaboration was on ownership of further improvements?

▸ In what ways was the Evaluative phase data used to inform further development, and/or to celebrate improvements?

GAS has been mentioned twice now so far: both Principal A and Sean used the tool and I have found it to be so useful that it is worthy of further discussion. GAS is a system for more objectively quantifying the achievement of goals (Molyneux, Koo, Piggot-Irvine, Talmage, Travaglia,

& Willis, 2012). It has mostly been associated with the health, particularly the mental health, sector but has more recently found its way into other sectors (see Latham & Locke, 2006; Roach & Elliott, 2005).

GAS involves establishing comprehensive criteria against which progress can be rated as 'expected' (neutral, 0, scoring), 'below expected' (-1 or -2 scoring), or 'above expected' (+1 or +2 scoring). An example of a GAS template for evaluating Sean's goal pursuit plans is provided in Table 3.4. Note the outcomes for each phase of FAR Model form horizontal categories and ratings form the vertical categories. This might look very complicated and I originally felt this categorization would require a lot of work. Having used GAS with many people, I no longer consider this to be the case. The measurable outcomes almost always transfer directly from the plan drawn up for goal pursuit so little work is involved in relocating them to the GAS table. The ratings statements themselves are reasonably standard and logical across GAS tables and again therefore little work is involved in constructing those also. For example, the neutral, 0, expected level is almost always the same wording as the measurable outcome statement on the action plan. The -1 level is at the 'limited' achievement level, or some similar synonym. The -2 level indicates no achievement etc. Sean's GAS in Table 3.4 illustrates such category construction.

Sean used the GAS as a self-review tool to enhance his objective analysis of the effectiveness of goal achievement. GAS is useful beyond just this level of self-review however. Bovend'Eerdt, Botell and Wade (2009) are clear that GAS should be used to encourage ongoing consultation between all associated with the goal. I prefer the word 'dialogue' to describe such 'consultation' and in the following chapter, the meaning of the term dialogue is provided. In Sean's case, he asked his teachers to rate his achievement and then engaged in dialogue with each teacher about the comparison of his and their ratings. Principal A encouraged teachers, students and caregivers/parents to each complete a GAS for the goals students developed to enhance learning focus and then they collectively compared ratings. I therefore advocate extending Bovend'Eerdt et al.'s description of 'consultation' and add that conversation about the GAS ratings between these parties involved in the goal pursuit creates a rich opportunity for deep dialogue and reflection about goal pursuit which, in turn, can be associated with extended ideas for further development.

TABLE 3.4 GAS for use with Sean's plans

Outcome Attainment Levels	Reconnaissance Outcome 1	Reconnaissance Outcome 2	Implementation Outcome	Evaluation Outcome 1	Evaluation Outcome 2
Most unfavourable outcomes (−2)	Effectiveness Criteria (EC) synthesized	Data gathered on the existing situation associated with report writing	Action plan developed, reflections on progress recorded	Evidence of improvement shown in marks and EC	Further refinement of EC synthesized
	No EC listed	No data collected, analysed or summarized. EC not used as reference for data collection.	No action plan developed, no reflections on progress recorded	No data shown or summarized. EC not used as reference for data collection.	No further review of EC
Less than expected success with outcomes (−1)	Brief &/or simplistic &/or synthesized &/or unrelated to report writing EC list	Limited evidence collected using EC	A limited action plan developed and limited reflections on progress recorded	Limited evidence collected using EC	Limited EC review
Expected level outcomes (0)	Synthesized list of EC focused on goal	Evidence collected, analysed and summarized associated with the EC	Action plan developed, reflections on progress recorded	Evidence collected, analysed and summarized associated with the EC	Review of EC
More than expected success with outcomes (+1)	Range of references/material drawn upon for synthesized EC list	More than two data sources provided as evidence collected, analysed and summarized associated with the EC	Enhanced, detailed, action plan developed, reflections on progress recorded in depth	More than two data sources provided as evidence collected, analysed and summarized associated with the EC	Detailed review of EC drawn up
Best anticipated success with outcomes (+2)	Extensive material synthesized and critiqued for synthesized EC list	Extensive data sources provided as evidence collected, analysed and summarized associated with the EC	Extensive action plan developed, and extensive, in depth, reflections on progress recorded	Extensive data sources provided as evidence collected, analysed and summarized associated with the EC	Extensive, enhanced, review of EC developed

GAS is seen to have multiple advantages and disadvantages which have been recorded by Roach and Elliott (2005: 15), as summarized in Table 3.5. The disadvantages are largely associated with a need for further research on this topic.

TABLE 3.5 Advantages and disadvantages of GAS ratings

Advantages of GAS Ratings	Disadvantages of GAS Ratings
• Time efficient • Personalized/ individual assessment • Conceptually consistent if behavioural consultation • Requires minimal skills to collect data • Non-intrusive assessment method • Can be used as a self-assessment • Can be used by multiple informants across settings (e.g., home, educational organization, community) • Can be used repeatedly to monitor perceptions of intervention progress • Can be used to document perceptions of intervention outcomes • Inexpensive • Requires minimal skills to interpret data	• Limited published, empirical, research on the education-based use of the method • Subjective summary of observations collected over time • Not norm-referenced • Guidelines for interpretation are determined by parties involved with the intervention, thus subject to bias • Global (i.e. less discrete) accounting of behaviour

To summarize for the Evaluation phase in goal pursuit, in the haste to move on to the next new idea for improvement, leaders often truncate or overlooked this phase altogether. However, in my observation, leaders who have been committed to sustained and deep level change that lifts performance have readily engaged in thoroughly examining the effectiveness of the improvements they have made before progressing to a new idea. They have also been open to becoming 'informed', or evidence based', in the Evaluation phase and have found this a strongly confirming activity that offers wonderful opportunity for celebration of achievement.

I have found that well-articulated anticipated, or expected, outcomes stated in the deep goal planning considerably assist with clarifying the approaches to evaluation.

After Evaluation phase activity in the FAR Model there is a drawing up of recommendations for further improvement derived from the analysis of the Evaluation phase findings and then reporting on the overall goal pursuit project.

Recommendations for further improvement and reporting achievement

Before discussing recommendation development and ways of sharing the goal pursuit achievement through reporting out, I want to emphasize that this Model includes a statement of 'continued action for improvement'. Though there is only one cycle of phased activity shown in the Model and although there are 'spin off cycles illustrated, there is an absolute expectation that iterative, continuing, cycles will occur with recommendations from one cycle leading into further refinement, deepening or elaboration. Sustaining improvements from one cycle to the next is critical.

I will focus on drawing up recommendations first as a key activity in this phase of the model. At the end of the previous Evaluation phase, the analysis of the data collected should have occurred followed by reflection on the implications of those findings. The recommendations for further improvement should be considerably derived from the findings. I strongly encourage the use of some form of engagement activity for the drawing up of recommendations. Such engagement is essential in order to gain the buy-in necessary for sustained implementation of improvement associated with the recommendations. Appelbaum and Wohl (2000) and Bushe and Marshak (2009) also urge the active participation of key individuals in shared decision making beyond just goal setting to that of initiation of sustainable action. My favourite recommendation development activity called 'Force Field Analysis' (FFA) is designed to actively involve others.

FFA is described and applied in varying ways but Coghlan and Brannick (2010), Weisbord (2012), and Schwering (2003) are the authors whose work I have drawn upon in developing my own interpretation of this activity. In FFA the outcome is to both share recommendations with those who are likely to be affected by improvements, or may influence their implementation, and also to ensure such people are part of the planning for such improvements. These key individuals work in small groups to help prioritize the recommendations (remember 'few things done well'), create desired outcomes for each prioritized recommendation, and brainstorm both the factors which will drive towards the ideal and those resistors that might detract from the ideal. Each factor is then weighted and a graphic drawn to show those weightings. Figure 3.2 shows a simple generic graphic. Note that a context specific graphic would have the brainstormed factors named alongside each arrow.

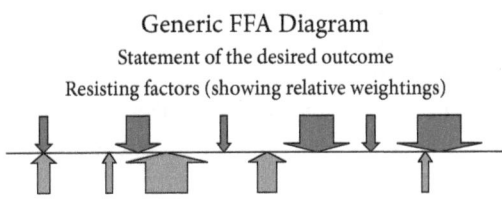

Generic FFA Diagram
Statement of the desired outcome
Resisting factors (showing relative weightings)

Factors driving the change forward (weighted)

FIGURE 3.2   *Force Field Analysis diagram*

In my experience, the drawing of the graphic for FFA helps make it very clear to participants which factors will need to be acted upon to drive them towards the desired outcome (i.e. the largest 'driver' arrow factors) and which will need to be reduced or minimized (the largest 'resistor' arrow factors). Small, usually self-selected groups, of the key individuals then collaborate to develop deep level action plans which incorporate the factors identified in the graphic in order to flesh out implementation steps that will ensure the 'desired outcomes' for each recommendation are achieved.

A more detailed outline of the steps in this process is provided in Chapter 6, but I want to reiterate that FFA is designed to ensure enhanced 'buy-in' of the recommendations via considerable collaboration of key individuals. I have repeatedly observed even the most resistant of these individuals moving to a strongly positive, supportive stance via the activity. The reason for this is linked primarily to two elements in the activity: the early brainstorming component when the graphic is developed and then the identification of what needs to be acted upon. In the brainstorming element the dialogue described as a component of authentic collaboration is highlighted as central to the brainstorm. I strongly encourage whoever is facilitating the FFA activity to preface the brainstorm task by coaching participants in how to engage in dialogue. In such an authentic collaborative milieu, participants air their positive and negative thoughts about the desired outcome and in doing so there is very frequently some shift to resolving resistance. The second element that encourages a move to a more positive stance often occurs in the identification of what needs to be acted upon at the later action planning stage. The emphasis at this stage is to include actions in the plan which maximize that driving factors and minimize the resistors. Both components of this emphasis are positive overall in approach and once again this positive stance helps resolve resistance.

I have observed remarkable engagement and 'buy-in' outcomes from FFA and this is therefore one of my pet tools in goal pursuit. I have employed this activity with groups of up to 50 people and with strong facilitation it can be one of the quickest ways to share goal pursuit outcomes with key individuals and also an exceptional approach for moving recommendations into practical action plans that have strong ownership. I usually encourage implementation of the tool before reporting on goal pursuit overall.

I have observed remarkable engagement and 'buy-in' outcomes from FFA and this is therefore one of my pet tools in goal pursuit.

Following drawing up of recommendations, the second key activity in the post-Evaluation phase of the FAR Model is reporting. In Chapter 2, I referred to Locke and Latham's (2013) finding that making goals public, i.e. sharing them with others, impacts on achievement of goals. However, such sharing does not just happen at the initial goal setting step. It occurs throughout the FAR Model, but it becomes particularly important after the Evaluation phase. The FAR goal pursuit model, like most AR (Piggot-Irvine & Bartlett, 2008), attends to sharing of impacts by incorporating an expectation that reporting of achievement and recommendations occurs as a post-Evaluation phase activity. Altrichter, Kemmis, McTaggart, and Zuber-Skerritt (2000) in fact assert that a defining feature of AR is that of making outcomes public to other people who are concerned by and interested in the practice. Public reporting does not necessarily mean circulating achievements and recommendations to everyone in an organization: principally it means sharing with those who are either impacted by the achievement or have a vested interested (such as a line manager, or an interested teacher, or other key stakeholders).

What I am suggesting here is that there should be some degree of organizational or public accountability in goal pursuit and this becomes most evident at the Recommendation and Reporting phase. Such accountability has three key purposes. The first is to enhance validity of the outcomes by opening them up to feedback and perhaps critique by others. The second purpose in sharing the achievements and recommendations with others is to allow the goal pursuer to reflect upon feedback, to rethink their ideas, and perhaps potentially enhance their practice. A third purpose is to enhance 'buy-in' from those who may need to be involved in recommendations for further improvements. With any of these activities the importance of authentic collaboration cannot be underestimated if goal pursuit is to be credible—a point that is given considerable attention in the following chapter.

> Consider your previous experiences with goal pursuit.
>
> ▸ How did reporting of achievement occur?
>
> ▸ In developing a reporting outline or recommendations for further improvement, in what ways did collaboration with key stakeholders occur?
>
> ▸ If collaboration occurred in this phase, did it enhance 'buy-in' from those who may have needed to be involved in recommendations for further improvements?

Reporting can occur in multiple ways whether at the end of each Phase of the FAR Model or toward the end of a full set of phases. I have seen reports written that range from a one to two page summary on achievements and recommendations through to a full blown report of anything up to 100 pages outlining detail of each of the phased processes and outcomes. An example of simple reflective questions for reporting is provided in Chapter 6. In summary, these cover: description of the organization; description of goal pursuit team; rationale for goal selection; a key phase overview diagram; key activities and outcomes for each phase; conclusions and recommendations; and an appendix of tools used.

If the goal in goal pursuit is organization wide rather than team or individually focused, usually the governing body determines the parameters of the reporting but it is the leaders who still most often write the report. If goals are set at a team level, usually the leader of the group writes the report. If set at an individual level either this person or their line manager writes the report. In all of these contexts, I encourage collaboration and joint writing with key stakeholders. Regardless of who writes the report, the type or length, an essential element in reporting is involvement and collaboration with others and extensive communication if ownership of the outcomes is to result. In the next chapter, the three key underpinning principles are discussed, and such authentic collaboration elaborated.

Summary

- The FAR Model includes Preparatory, Reconnaissance, Implementation, Evaluation, Recommendation development and Reporting phases. Multiple cycles of these phases are likely.
- In preparing for goal pursuit, clarifying underpinning principles is important, as is alignment of priorities to national, regional and local contextually set goals, along with resource allocation to enable each phase of goal pursuit.
- In the Reconnaissance (current situation analysis) phase there should be both rigorous data collection using multiple tools/methods alongside becoming 'informed' about other research and findings on the specific goal. A final component of this phase is collaborative development of a deep level plan for improvement resulting from reflection on these 'findings'.
- In the Implementation phase the plan for improvement is carried out.
- In the Evaluation phase, as with the Reconnaissance phase, rigorous data collection on the outcomes, impacts, and effectiveness of the improvements occurs. Collaborative analysis and reflection upon the findings is essential for ensuring ownership of further, deeply planned, sustained improvements.
- In drawing up recommendations strong and authentic collaboration is needed to ensure that buy-in occurs for further actions. Reporting is an essential element of the Model that enhances public accountability and celebration of the outcomes.

4
How the FAR Model Encourages Shift in Depth, Lift in Challenge, and Collaboration

Abstract: *Chapter 4 covers the three underpinning principles of the FAR Model. The rationale for 'shift' in depth and `lift' in challenge is offered, followed by detailed elaboration of 'authentic collaboration' as a central feature of effective goal pursuit. 'Shift' in depth can lead to greater focus and enhanced outcomes and impact. Depth is initially created via deep goal pursuit plan construction that essentially mirrors a mini AR approach with phased activity. 'Lift' in goal pursuit is associated with enhanced performance and outcomes – the higher the goal, the higher the performance. Lift in goals occurs when stretch, or challenge, goals are set rather than easy to achieve goals. Authentic collaboration is the underpinning which I consider to hold more significance to success than any other element. I attempt to show not only the defensive strategies and values preventing authentic collaboration but also what can be `productively' implemented to enhance it.*

Keywords: advocacy; authentic collaboration; defensive strategies; dialogue; inquiry; lift in challenge; , productive strategies; shift in depth

Piggot-Irvine, Eileen. *Goal Pursuit in Education Using Focused Action Research*. New York: Palgrave Macmillan, 2015. DOI: 10.1057/9781137505125.0009.

Introduction

The FAR Model is designed to create deep and challenging improvement, or what I describe as the principles of 'shift' and 'lift' in goal pursuit. In all of my work I strive to get the best possible outcomes, whether from leaders, graduate students, students of all ages, or teachers. Getting best possible outcomes also often means that I quite persistently need to introduce specificity and challenge so that both a shift in depth and lift in thinking and action occur. It is my experience that goal pursuit is best enacted when participants are engaged with others in ways where not only support, clarity, and mentoring is provided but also strong feedback, honest dialogue, and critique: all features of what I am describe as authentic collaboration. The underpinning principles of shift, lift, and authentic collaboration are covered in this chapter and as you read this material recall that a 'growth mind-set' with a development, or improvement, intent is central to each underpinning principle.

'Shift in depth' in goal pursuit

In order to create focus and meaningful actions and outcomes in goal pursuit I encourage (and dare I say 'expect') what I am going to describe as 'deep' goal setting and planning. 'Deep' can be contrasted with 'surface' (Piggot-Irvine, 2003). A surface approach to goal pursuit is a quick-fix strategy and one concerned with getting the goal completed in an expedient way rather than focusing substantially on considerable improvement. It conforms to a 'surface learning' approach which McKay and Kember (1997) state, is "based on a motive to minimise effort and also to minimise the consequences" (p. 58). I have seen many goals articulated and pursued in such a surface way as the following example will show.

A 'surface' then 'shift to depth' example

At the beginning of a consultancy contract, a leader I worked with showed me one goal he had set for the school for the year. The goal title was: 'To improve the performance review system'. This was quite a laudable goal and could be, in fact is frequently, a challenging goal which can lead to impressive substantial organizational improvement. In the early stages of working with this particular leader, however, he had written just the following three lines as descriptors for the pursuit and outcomes for this goal:

- Rewrite the performance review forms into a clearer format;
- Have a meeting with staff to tell them about the new forms; and
- Roll out the forms for the following year review process.

These goal descriptors show no evidence of any examination of what might currently be working (or not) in the performance review system, no use of evidence to support any improvements to be made, no examination of any literature or best practice ideas on what constitutes an effective review system, no attempt to involve or collaborate with key stakeholders in order to create engagement or 'buy-in' for changes, no detail of improvements that would be introduced or any timeline or expected outcomes, and no outline of how the quality of any improvements would be evaluated. In sum, this example fits a 'surface' approach to goal pursuit. It would have involved minimal effort on the part of the leader, but also would have had minimal improvement outcomes.

I worked with this leader over several sessions to shift the goal descriptors to fit a 'deep' goal format. 'Deep' refers to goal pursuit which includes all of the things outlined that the surface plan was missing. It has:

- examination of what is currently be working (or not) in the focus area of the goal;
- use of evidence/data to support any conclusions drawn in the analysis of the current situation;
- becoming informed through examination of any literature or best practice ideas on what constitutes an effective system linked to the goal;
- sharing of the findings with key stakeholders to ensure involvement and collaboration in order to create engagement or 'buy-in' for potential changes, improvements to be made;
- detailed planning to show improvement steps, timelines, outcomes, that might be introduced associated with the goal;
- a phase of well-planned, evidence/data-based evaluation of the quality of any improvements made; and
- an outline of how findings from the evaluation would be shared and reported upon and how key stakeholders would be involved in developing recommendations.

> Consider your previous experiences with goal pursuit.
>
> ▸ How well did the overall plan for goal pursuit in your experience match the list of descriptors outlined here for deep planning?
>
> ▸ If either the plan did, or did not, match these descriptors, what impact did this depth (or lack of it) have on subsequent activity and outcomes in the goal pursuit?

A shift to 'deep' goal pursuit, as noted in Chapter 1, is in effect a shift to a small AR, inquiry learning, type project (Piggot-Irvine & Bartlett, 2008; Piggot-Irvine et al., 2011), such as that outlined in the FAR Model in Chapter 3. As noted in the previous chapter, evidence-based decision making is critical in shifting to such a deep approach, as is detailed planning and reflection associated with action.

Table 3.2 in Chapter 3 details how Sean, a student, both engaged in the activities of the FAR Model for goal pursuit, as well as wrote a plan for the way he conducted this. I described this as an example of deep goal pursuit and planning. I can report also that in an interview with Sean he described his deep goal pursuit approach as strongly motivating for him and I contend this is potentially because it met the Robinson et al. (2009) conditions for motivating goals in an education setting. First, Sean felt he had the capacity to meet the goal and had the resources (expertise and support) required. Second, he was committed—primarily because he actually chose and planned the goal. Third, the goal was specific and unambiguous—his plan was written in a way that showed him how to assess progress. Fourth, Sean's goal may also have been motivating because it helped him move from an abstract idea to concrete and practical action steps for improvement as well as being focused on skill and knowledge acquisition. You will perhaps notice this matches the 'Integration' element referred to earlier in the AIM model in neuroleadership work (Berkman & Rock, 2012) where both 'how' and 'why' thinking is encouraged. Such aspects are also noted as important characteristics of both 'performance' and 'learning' goals by Latham and Locke (2003).

Another example from a school leader goal should further illustrate what an overall deep plan might look like, as shown in Table 4.1. In this example, a senior leader had chosen as a personal performance review goal that he wanted to improve his facilitation of meetings.

In the shift to 'depth' in goal pursuit I strongly encourage 'doing few things and doing them well'. In my experience, well thought out goals seem to lead to much greater levels of focus, motivation, and achievement. There is a consideration to be taken into account with such focus, however, as highlighted in a study by Simons and Chabris (1999). These authors have shown that when there is too much focus there can be an outcome of bias in terms of missing other aspects of the job. Expressed in another way, too much focus can create tunnel vision rather than seeing the whole picture of the goal and its link to wider aspects of a role.

I strongly encourage "doing few things and doing them well". In my experience, well thought out goals seem to lead to much greater levels of focus, motivation and achievement.

'Lift' in goal pursuit

Lift in thinking and action with goals is frequently associated with the term 'high' (sometimes also called 'stretch') goals. Locke and Latham's (2013) recent work provides an exceptionally clear overview of the importance of high goals. Such goals are suggested to focus an individual's attention and effort towards goal-oriented activity and away from irrelevant activity. They are goals that activate the knowledge and skills necessary to attain the goal. Latham and Locke (2006) note: "... setting high goals means setting the bar higher ... the higher the goal, the higher the performance" (p. 333). Though, as noted in Chapter 2, I have some caution about drawing absolute conclusions from the neuroleadership material, Whiting, Jones, Rock and Bendit (2013) report from this field also the importance of having stretch and specific goals for inspiring new ideas.

We know from other research that high goals have benefits of leading people to work harder and longer than an easy goal. As early as 1967, Locke showed a linear relationship between goal difficulty and

TABLE 4.1 An example of deep level plan

Goal	Actions	Measurable Outcomes	Resources/s (Recorded for each action)	Date for Completion
To improve the way that I facilitate meetings with staff so that I don't waste valuable time.	*Reconnaissance* 1. Do some reading on meeting facilitation and develop criteria for effectiveness	• Knowledge of effective meeting facilitation, and a clear set of criteria for this	1. Photocopying of articles $5.00	April 20th

	Current Situation Analysis
	2. Check how I facilitate meetings currently against the criteria by:
	  a. asking staff to complete a quick response questionnaire on my effectiveness
	  b. asking a colleague to observe and record what I do in meetings
		• A summary of findings from feedback and observation	2 a Photocopying of questionnaire $5.00
			2 b Nil
				April 30th

	Planning for Improvement 3. Think about the results from the feedback etc. and develop a plan for the way I will improve	• Implementation plan developed	3. Nil	June 1st
	Carrying out Plan 4. Attend a 2–hour workshop on meeting facilitation	• Notes taken at workshop	4. Workshop fee $200.00 Travel $20.00	June 15th
	5. Observe another manager who is reputed to facilitate good meetings	• Observation notes made	5. Nil	June 20th
	6. Put my plan for improved facilitation into practice for 2–3 meetings, followed by feedback from a colleague as observer, then further improvement to facilitation implemented for 2–3 meetings	• Incremental improvement shown as recorded in observation and feedback from my observer colleague	6. Nil	June 25th To ... July 25th
	Evaluation 7. Seek further feedback from staff on improvements, and ask my colleague to conduct a final observation against my criteria for effective facilitation	• Analysis of observation and feedback shows areas of improvement and recommendations for further improvement	7. Photocopying of survey $5.00	End July

performance (see Locke & Latham, 2013), noting that people with the highest (more difficult and challenging) goals had 25 percent increases in performance over those with easy goals. The intensity of a goal, the amount of thought and mental effort involved in setting high goals, is seen to affect commitment to the goal, and in my interpretation, therefore achievement. Tubbs (1986) and Mento, Steel and Karren (1987) have also provided evidence of a positive correlation between specific, difficult goals and improved performance.

There is some caution here however. Goals which are too high, too difficult and unachievable can cause people to be demoralized and demotivated. Further, Ordóñez and Scheitzer (2004) consider that people may have a tendency to be dishonest if they do not achieve their goals. It is important to consider such cautions around lifting goals to too high a level, particularly when Sitkin, See, Miller, Lawless and Carton (2011) inform us there has been underreporting of the counter-productive effects of 'stretch' goals.

An 'easy' then 'lift to high' example

A senior leader in a large regional office showed me the following goal chosen by a team leader for her team for the year: 'To create and share a filing system to record staff contact details'. Apart from the fact that this goal did not cascade from any organizational goal, it met none of the criteria for a high, stretch, or challenging goal. It would have activated little knowledge or skill for either the leader or her team. It would not have led individuals to work harder or longer, and would have required little thought or mental effort. I would hardly have classified this as an easy goal; rather it was a simple administrative task.

I coached this senior leader to engage in a dialogue with the team leader to help her to recognize the difference between easy and high goals and to use her own new knowledge of deepening and lifting goals in this dialogue. The senior leader had created a goal for 'enhancing appreciation of staff' that had not only a fully fleshed out AR based deep plan, but also showed a focus with all the hallmarks of challenge and stretch: in other words a high goal that was activating him to engage in considerable thought and effort to develop the knowledge and skill for achievement of the goal.

> Consider your previous experiences with goal pursuit.
>
> ▸ How challenging was the goal set in terms of creating stretch and 'lift'?
>
> ▸ If either the goal was, or was not, challenging what impact did this (or lack of it) have on subsequent activity and outcomes in the goal pursuit?

Before finishing this discussion of 'lift' I want to take a moment to recount the initial response of many people I have introduced this approach to. The underpinnings of 'shift' and 'lift' have required a considerable movement in thinking and practice for almost all of these people and with such change there has often been a predictable resistance response. In order to alleviate this resistance I am exceptionally careful early in the discussion of goal pursuit to show examples of what 'surface' and 'deep' plans look like. I also gently introduce some theory on the shifts in learning and quality of outcomes that can result. I assure individuals and teams that I will work alongside them in every stage of planning and actioning the deeper approach to goal pursuit. With this support, most people I have worked with have been willing to try the shift to a deeper approach and lift in expectations.

Admittedly, however, two people I have introduced this approach to have been more resistant and the school leader with the 'surface' goal example shown earlier in this chapter was an example of someone who showed such resistance. When I engaged in my somewhat supportive approach I have described, in his words the leader stated that he thought this shift was "... too academic for the organization ... over the top in terms of detail". I did get him to agree to think about it a bit more in the couple of weeks before our next meeting and suggested he might want to think also about just 'trialling' the approach for only one goal. He came back to the next meeting with a fairly grudging agreement to the trial but over the time of his goal pursuit, despite my support, the resistance still emerged on a regular basis. At the end of the year, after the Evaluation phase had been completed, he stunned me however with the following comment he made in a public forum: "... she was dogged about this "deep goal" approach being better and I tell you I went into it kicking and screaming but now I am going to roll this out for all team goals as well. I tell you, it worked". Given that ultimate recommendation, I want to share with you my bottom line if you adopt this approach. If you want to introduce the shift and lift in this approach with others you will need to have a bit of dogged determination. One of my students described me in her thesis acknowledgement as the "loving ankle-biter". I confess to this being pretty accurate, but I also want to suggest that you will also need to be compassionately determined if you want to see results from the approach!

> *If you want to introduce the shift and lift in this approach with others you will need to have a bit of dogged determination.*

Authentic collaboration and feedback

As noted repeatedly through the previous chapters, collaboration in goal pursuit is critical if 'buy-in', ownership, and engagement is to occur for all those affected. Collaboration occurs at multiple points.

In the Preparatory phase in the FAR Model, the activity of selection of goals usually involves several people determining which goal(s) are appropriate. Even at an individual level people often seek input and advice from others before making a choice about which goal(s) to focus on. Recently, I observed an exceptional example of collaboration at the Preparatory phase when the CEO invited staff to offer indications of a goal they wished to see him focus on. From those offerings he then chose one goal matching the majority of wishes. Of course, he also had a variety of other goals that matched the strategic objectives of the organization, but his openness to seeking feedback from staff won him considerable respect from them.

In the Reconnaissance, Implementation, Evaluation, Recommendation and Reporting phases of the FAR goal pursuit Model, as noted earlier in this book, I strongly urge engaging key others to ensure ownership of improvements and further actions. I have also suggested that inviting feedback from others throughout goal pursuit enhances openness to new ideas. In almost all goal pursuit activity I encourage goal pursuers to set up a relationship with one or two others where ongoing and regular dialogue occurs about goal achievement.

For example, in School A, a powerful triad relationship between each student, their teacher, and caregivers was established for student goals and this triad met approximately monthly to ensure regular feedback and support was provided.

The neuroleadership writing from Uhl-Bein and Marion (2009) emphasizes the importance of such sharing of ideas and knowledge, and they point out how this leads to different ideas merging, diverging and elaborating. Berkman and Rock (2012), and Ringleb and Rock (2013) note such sharing of ideas and collaboration as a critical 'approach' condition in the 'relatedness' element in the SCARF Model, and in the AIM Model it falls under the 'social context' antecedent, as described in Chapter 2.

Feedback on goals might occur from peers, leaders, or other key stakeholders. In performance review, the feedback is often summative, or end-point, from the reviewer who is usually in a hierarchically superior position. Though such summative feedback can also occur at the final phase of goal pursuit, throughout many phases of the process feedback is of a more formative, ongoing and developmental, intent.

Feedback is not only important for ongoing motivation in goal pursuit but also for overall progression, goal modification when needed, and achievement. As Sorrentino (2006) has reported, feedback helps in determining the level of effort required in goal pursuit. Locke and Latham (2013) suggest that effort in fact increases (i.e. we try harder) when there is an indication we are not fully achieving a goal: feedback provides that indication. Locke and Latham (2013) particularly note the importance of personalizing recognition and feedback.

Seeking input, engaging others, and inviting feedback all involve collaboration at some level. I am going to suggest that all collaboration in fact is not equal! I encourage 'authentic' collaboration and it is this topic I now focus upon as the third principle underpinning the FAR Model.

I want to begin by clarifying the term 'collaboration' itself. 'Co-labour' implies joint work; however variable terms are frequently associated, and sometimes used interchangeably, with collaboration—terms such as consultation, involvement, participation, partnership, cooperation, agreement and consent. Collaboration is variably interpreted. Further, unlike Hattori and Lapidus (2004), who imply in a case study they cite that trust is a *precondition for* collaboration, I suggest it is a *consequence of* collaboration: in fact a "hard earned outcome from effective collaboration" (Piggot-Irvine, 2012: 91).

Consider your previous experiences with goal pursuit.

- To what extent were formative (on-going, developmental) and summative (end-point) feedback elements incorporated in the goal pursuit process?
- Describe the approach to collaboration that was engaged in throughout.
- How do you consider the approach adopted might have impacted on the success of the goal pursuit process?

Collaboration necessitates highly skilled co-labourers if it is to be effective in goal pursuit and of critical importance in trust development is the adoption of a dialogic stance. There are many interpretations of dialogue, but I like that of MacKeracher (2004) who says that dialogue:

> ...whether carried out internally with oneself or externally with others... explores alternative viewpoints in order to develop an integrated viewpoint synthesized from the best aspects of alternatives (p. 8).

MacKeracher tightly distils what I have described (Piggot-Irvine, 2012) as associated with the deepest level of collaboration: a level I have claimed to be *authentic*. Such collaboration involves genuinely expressing a viewpoint but also equally listening to the viewpoint of others so that great outcomes are achieved. Unfortunately I have not always observed such authentic collaboration in my work in goal pursuit. In contrast, I have repeatedly experienced, and sadly sometimes practised myself, inauthentic collaboration. It is important to examine more closely at what inauthentic and authentic collaboration look like.

Inauthentic and authentic collaboration

I am going to start with inauthentic collaboration because it is the approach that I am well aware that I can get caught up in. Often when I have been inauthentic it has never been intentional and I have sometimes been considerably ignorant of it occurring, an ignorance described as common by the esteemed authors Argyris and Schön (1974).

Inauthentic collaboration, in my view, falls under the realm of 'defensiveness'—a common and predominant response when there is threat or difference of opinion (Argyris & Schön, 1974). Argyris (2003) defines defensiveness as the tendency to protect ourselves and others from potential threat and embarrassment. In feedback in a goal pursuit context, or any other pressured context for that matter, there is an almost inevitable threatened, defensive response if the feedback is poorly facilitated.

Inauthentic collaboration, in my view, falls under the realm of "defensiveness" - a common and predominant response when there is threat or difference of opinion (Argyris & Schön, 1974).

Avoidance and control are the two key strategies of defensiveness. In a tense context, for example, 'protection' (of ourselves and others) often dominates and includes us covering up or withholding vital information/evidence when we feel it would 'hurt' others. This is an *avoidance* strategy. Alternatively, or frequently additionally, in such tense contexts we are also often indirect by giving mixed rather than clear messages (this is potentially either *avoidance or control*). Or sometimes we aggressively confront others with our opinion but with low levels of evidence (strongly *controlling*). In each of these situations, even in avoidance, decision making is controlled by the person giving feedback or input and minimal collaboration occurs. For example, if a leader is excessive in stating their own perspective when giving feedback about progress with a goal but does not allow significant response from the goal pursuer, they are defensively *unilaterally controlling* the feedback: in other words it is 'one-sided' feedback.

Alternatively, in authentic collaboration, there is striving for shared (*bilateral*) control through everyone employing what is sometimes called a non-defensive or 'productive' orientation (Argyris, 2003; Cardno, 2001; Senge, Cambron-McCabe, Lucas, Smith, Dutton & Kleiner, 2000). Here, a more consensual approach to collaboration is adopted involving a balance of articulation of evidence and reasoning (thinking behind what is being said) linked to observations and perceptions (*advocacy*) alongside invitation for careful checking and open understanding of others' perspectives without prejudgement (*inquiry*). There is a very fine balancing act to ensure that neither advocacy nor inquiry dominate, as shown in Figure 4.1.

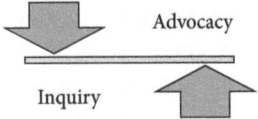

FIGURE 4.1 *Balancing advocacy and inquiry*

If either over-advocacy or over-inquiry occurs then defensive domination and control are evident. If under-advocacy or under-inquiry occurs then defensive avoidance is evident. With advocacy and inquiry in balance, a two-way conversation or *dialogue* results leading to mutual understanding and agreement (or agreement to disagree) about shared evidence (see Piggot-Irvine & Doyle, 2010, for detailed elaboration on elements of dialogue). Preskill and Torres (1999) suggest through dialogue:

> ...individuals seek to inquire, share meanings, understand complex issues, and uncover assumptions. In other words, dialogue is what facilitates the...learning processes of reflection, asking questions, and identifying and clarifying values, beliefs, assumptions and knowledge... (p. 53).

What does this look like in practice in a goal pursuit context? I will use an example to illustrate this. I encourage the person providing feedback to emphasize showing the goal pursuer objective evidence of achievement (*advocacy*) rather than offering opinion. This is followed by the person giving feedback then enabling the pursuer to draw their own conclusions from the evidence using strong clarifying and probing questions (*inquiry*) and listening skills. In this way the goal pursuer has control and ownership of the feedback process and is much less likely to become defensive.

> Consider your previous experiences with collaboration in goal pursuit.
>
> ▸ To what extent was defensiveness (on the part of the provider of feeder or the goal pursuer) present when feedback was provided?
>
> ▸ If present, describe what that defensiveness looked like in terms of advocacy and inquiry.
>
> ▸ What strategies might have been introduced to create enhanced authentic collaboration where dialogue featured?

Following the balanced advocacy and inquiry, i.e. dialogue in providing feedback in goal pursuit, there are further components involved in progressing towards authentic collaboration. A key component is for the pursuer to *prioritize next steps in their goal pursuit*. Once again, it is critical the pursuer holds the responsibility for this prioritizing and creating their own insights, but the colleague providing feedback has a key role in using good inquiry (questioning, probing, reflecting, listening) to assist in clarifying thinking. In this way the goal pursuer once again has control and ownership of the priorities and the subsequent thinking about how the priorities will be actioned, and they are much less likely to be defensive in the process. Overall, the approach I am describing is solution-focused with a high degree of emphasis on 'ownership' and 'self-directness' of the goal pursuer. Further, this approach has been shown to have considerable impact on outcomes as I have shown in analysis of feedback (Piggot-Irvine, 2010).

> *... it is critical the pursuer holds the responsibility for this prioritizing and creating their own insights, but the colleague providing feedback has a key role in using good inquiry (questioning, probing, reflecting, listening) to assist in clarifying thinking.*

I have been striving to adopt this non-defensive, more productive, bilateral, and dialogical stance for the last two decades and along with a colleague (McMorland & Piggot-Irvine, 2000) part of our learning in this struggle has been to clarify our thinking about interactive challenges in collaboration from superficial, defensive types of collaboration through to what the ideal, or deepest, level of dialogue might look like. A hierarchy of collaboration levels resulted.

Levels of authentic collaboration

Recently, I further adapted (Piggot-Irvine, 2012) the earlier deepening levels of collaborative challenge that Judith McMorland and I created. The adaptation shows progression from superficial (Level 1) to the deepest, authentic type (Level 5) of collaboration. At the deepest level (5) there is openness that generates trust, as shown in Table 4.2.

TABLE 4.2 *Deepening levels of interactive challenge in collaboration*

Level	Challenges of Interaction
Level 1	*Introduction* (seeking and enjoying exploring commonality, excluding discussion of difference, collaborating in a superficial and task-specific way, and with little demonstration or examination of defensive values or strategies)
Level 2	*Recognition of potential of self and others* (with rising awareness of differential between self and others, waning enthusiasm for exploring commonality, and increasing willingness to entertain multilateral perspectives on reality, but action is usually limited despite personal perceptions of the value of self-contribution, and if doubt arises the response action is likely to be defensive and self-protective)
Level 3	*Gaining an inquiry perspective* (increasing empathy for the perception of others, and coming to genuine acceptance of the validity of another's way of being/thinking, seeing the world through others' eyes)
Level 4	*Transition to collaboration* (suspending one's own known perceptions and opening up to unknown other perceptions while allowing for exploration of creativity, true inquiry, and genuine collaborative action)
Level 5	*Trust and co-generation* (achieving new levels of awareness of both our own and others' perspectives, emerging as courage is expressed and inquiry leads to action—a process distinguished by spontaneity, synergy and creativity, and leading to openness, trust, and learning)

Source: Adapted from Piggot-Irvine, 2012: 94.

I also graphically interpreted these levels as shown in Figure 4.2. Note that although the figure illustrates multiple participants in collaboration in some levels, the principles apply equally when there are two people collaborating, such as in a feedback situation in goal pursuit.

I believe, and I have shown this in development with many people, the deeper levels of non-defensive, authentic collaboration in goal pursuit associated with trust and co-generation involve skills which can be learnt.

Attendant skills for authentic collaboration

Acquiring the deepest, trust engendering, dialogic openness shown in Level 5 in the Figure 4.2 is far from easy because most of us have been conditioned to a defensive response and changing from such a response is difficult, as noted by Piggot-Irvine and Doyle (2010):

> ... it requires significant, profound shifts involving exposure, examination and alteration of defensive values at a deeply personal level which is both cognitively and emotionally difficult and is a lengthy process. ... the approach

FIGURE 4.2 *Graphic representation of deepening levels of interactive challenge in collaboration*

Source: Adapted from Piggot-Irvine, 2012: 95.

> on its own is extremely complex and usually involves months, maybe years, of training. The reason for this is that the approach requires rethinking and altering our underlying value systems, and this involves changing many automatic, conditioned responses. Such values and responses cannot be changed in two hours! (p. 61)

I will use an example to show how these skills were employed with a group of education facilitators who had set a team goal to pilot a leadership development program in an organization. As part of their action plan, the group noted they would not only collect summative (endpoint) feedback from all participants on the program but also engage in collaborative intensive formative (ongoing) feedback with each other at the end of each unit in the program. In this formative feedback they particularly wanted to detect and correct gaps that may have existed between what Argyris and Schön (1974) term espousals (pre-determined program goals, aims, and curriculum) and practice (the facilitated program). Observation of each other's facilitation and documentary analysis (espoused session objectives, plans, content, process outlines, outcomes etc.) were used as evidence in the dialogue the team engaged in for each of their formative feedback sessions.

Prior to any of this dialogue occurring, however, the group worked with me over several intensive sessions to learn the skills required for authentic collaboration at the Level 5 shown in Figure 4.2. In particular I encourage them to be as open as possible by:

- using evidence rather than assumptions about the observation (an *advocacy* tool);
- coming to the point quickly if there was any concern with the evidence rather than 'easing in' with information (an *advocacy* tool);
- checking their interpretation of evidence continuously and acknowledging when they may have misinterpreted information (*inquiry*);
- trying to allow each facilitator to respond with input (*inquiry*);
- using open-ended questioning, paraphrasing, and listening skills (*inquiry*);
- constantly seeking explanations for any espousal-practice gap (*inquiry*); and
- progressing the dialogue by moving to 'next steps' including clarifying they had mutual understanding about what was observed and documented, and identifying and prioritizing improvements by finding mutually acceptable solutions (including checking of intended and unintended consequences).

As an observer of this approach, I can report that although espousal-practice gaps frequently existed in the facilitation there was not a single situation when a facilitator failed to identify the gap in the dialogue or, if they had not identified it, they were quick to recognize it when another facilitator who observed showed the evidence of the gap. In other words, there was a very low level of defensive response within the facilitator team.

The steps I have been describing for achieving dialogue in authentic collaboration have been reported in Piggot-Irvine (2012), and are shown in Table 4.3.

TABLE 4.3   *Dialogue steps for achieving authentic collaboration*

1. State your perception in a hypothetical way, i.e. open for challenge and checking.
2. Provide evidence for your perception.
3. Outline your reasoning and rationale for your perception. Collectively, Steps 1, 2 & 3 are often referred to as 'Advocacy' Steps.
4. Seek responses [check what others think, feel and perceive] without being defensive. This step is often referred to as the 'Inquiry' Step.
5. Summarize shared understanding or the need for more information and determine if there is an espousal—practice gap.

Repeat steps 1–5 if necessary before moving on.

6. Jointly suggest and evaluate solutions.
7. Decide together on a solution(s).

Source: Adapted from Piggot-Irvine, 2012: 100.

There are multiple skills associated with the steps described in Table 4.3 and you are referred to elaboration in Piggot-Irvine & Doyle (2010). The steps include:

▸ Withholding assumptions by staying low on a 'ladder of inference' (Senge et al., 2000);
▸ Reflecting-in-action and retrospectively reflecting-on-action (Schön,1983); and
▸ Engaging in double-loop learning (Argyris & Schön, 1996) i.e. examining and changing underlying defensive strategies and values.

> Think more broadly now about any previous experience where collaboration was intended.
>
> ▸ Overall, which level of interactive challenge was evident and why did you chose that level?
>
> ▸ If not at Level 5, what skills and process steps might have been introduced, implemented, in order to create a Level 5 type of collaboration?

I have experienced that where the skills and the dialogue steps for authentic collaboration have been implemented in goal pursuit, there have been enhanced outcomes associated with engagement of all of those collaborating, motivation and commitment to achievement. Most importantly, I have observed high levels of trust resultant from this authentic collaboration. The case study discussed in the next chapter is a fine example of where each of these outcomes eventuated in goal pursuit.

Summary

- 'Shift' in depth in goal pursuit can lead to greater focus and enhanced outcomes and impact. Depth is initially created via 'deep' goal pursuit plan construction that essentially mirrors a mini AR approach with phased activity. It also involves doing fewer things and doing them well.
- 'Lift' in goal pursuit is associated with enhanced performance and outcomes ... the higher the goal, the higher the performance. Lift in goals occurs when stretch, or challenge, goals are set rather than easy to achieve goals.
- Authentic collaboration is critical in almost every phase of the FAR Model. Such collaboration is associated with non-defensive interactions.
- Dialogue is apparent in feedback in authentic collaboration where a balance of advocacy and inquiry creates non-controlling and non-avoiding interactions.
- Multiple skills and process steps are associated with authentic collaboration, including withholding assumptions, strong reflection, and double-loop learning where underlying issues are explored.
- The outcome of consistent employment of the skills and steps associated with authentic collaboration is high trust.

5
What This Looks Like in a Real Case Study

Abstract: *Chapter 5 includes a real school case study to illustrate all phases of the FAR Model. Goal pursuit in this school is considered as meta-level because a school-wide goal was set for the topic of improving goal pursuit itself within the whole school. It is not a highly sophisticated, nor perfect (such a case does not exist), example but it does show application in context. The FAR Model activity engaged in matched current thinking and research associated with goal setting and achievement. In particular, and unusual in my experience, this school progressed to 'evaluation' as a confirming, consolidating, phase of the model and in doing so showed valuable evidence of successful implementation, celebrated achievement and most importantly were well-informed to clarify the next steps for improvement. This chapter concludes with discussion of drawing up recommendations and reporting on goal pursuit whilst employing collaboration to ensure engagement and buy-in from key people.*

Keywords: case study school; collaboration to ensure engagement; importance of evaluation; meta-level goal pursuit

Piggot-Irvine, Eileen. *Goal Pursuit in Education Using Focused Action Research*. New York: Palgrave Macmillan, 2015. DOI: 10.1057/9781137505125.0010.

Introduction

Every element of goal pursuit outlined so far can also be utilised at a 'meta', organization-wide level. The example I am outlining in this chapter demonstrates application at this level within a whole school. I have chosen the case because it is the best example of meta-level goal pursuit I have experienced. Very few of the hundreds of education sector organizations I have worked with in goal pursuit have attempted full, organization-wide, FAR Model implementation...or fully cascaded goal pursuit with any other model that I have observed. Even more concerning, those few organizations which have attempted the 'meta' level approach, have all introduced the cascading of goals in a highly unilateral, top-down, way with a consequence of poor engagement of those associated with the goals. I will use School A as a case study that illustrates well implementation of the FAR Model.

Case study

The case study I am using is of Principal A and her school (School A). Of course, you will note that I have mentioned this principal and school previously. In this chapter, however, I will show a complete picture of the way she used the FAR Model for goal pursuit. As an overview, Figure 5.1 shows the key content of the phases in the FAR Model employed in School A.

This meta, school-wide level goal pursuit began by cascading the principal's own performance review goal from that of a regional initiative which was stated as: 'to strengthen student learning via enhanced focus on specific, individualized, improvement goals; and enhance school-caregiver/parent interaction in improving student learning'. The Board of Governors chose as a more local goal: 'to "focus" learning for all students in a way that created stronger links between the school and caregivers/parents'. Figure 5.2 shows the cascading of the goal.

Most importantly, not only did the goals cascade and align, they also followed the FAR Model for goal pursuit outline. The principal, teachers and students alike had goals showing shift in depth and had lift in terms of being stretched to higher goals. In Principal A's personal performance review action plan, for example, she:

- intended overall goal *focus* for parents/caregivers, students and teachers, and ultimately the school to establish goal pursuit for improved student achievement in every classroom;

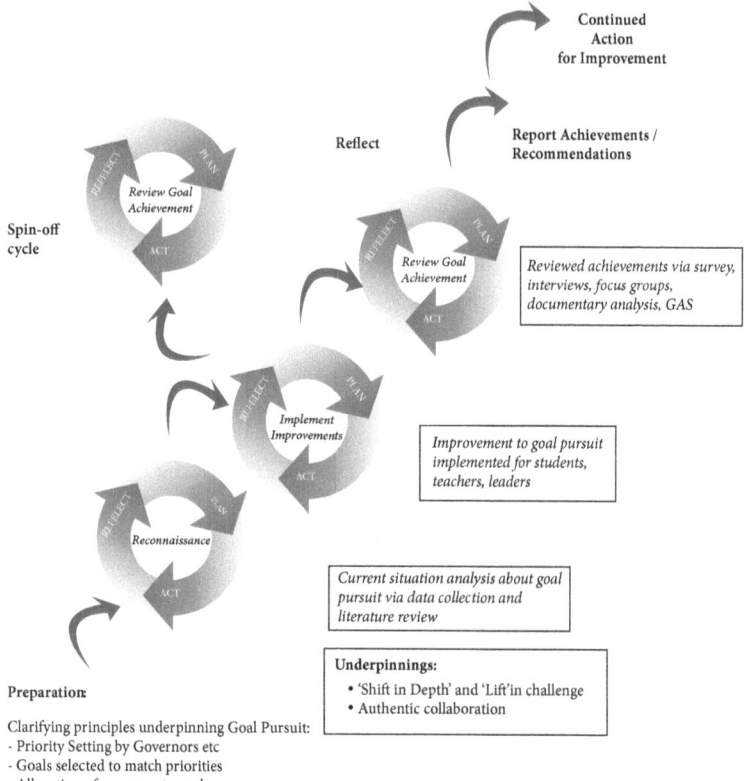

FIGURE 5.1 *The FAR Model in School A*
Source: Adapted from Piggot-Irvine, 2009.

- followed the selection of goals with alignment of resources to ensure goal achievement. She continuously provided leadership guidance and direction setting, financial support (particularly in time release) for goal pursuit, and mentoring or professional development if required;
- began by first carrying out an extensive *Reconnaissance* to collect data on the extent of goal setting currently in place in the school. She also established EC by working in a collaborative way to carry out a literature review on effective goal pursuit. In this way she enhanced engagement and motivation of the teachers in the task;

What This Looks Like in a Real Case Study 79

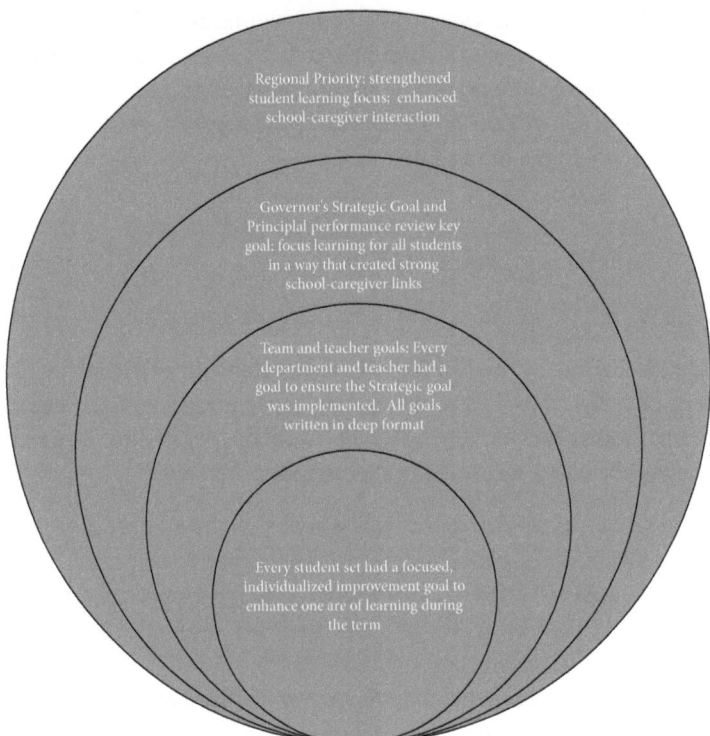

FIGURE 5.2   *Cascading of goals in School A*

- initiated the *Implementation* phase by undertaking considerable personal development to become fully informed about both implementing a major change and learning the detail of goal pursuit and its monitoring. She then used extensive collaboration, consultation and development processes to ensure that staff, students and their parents/caregivers were equally informed and involved in the planning and roll-out of this considerable initiative for all students to set goals to improve achievement. Further, she ensured sufficient resources were in place to support the achievement of this meta-goal;
- ensured in the *Implementation* phase that every child set a challenging learning goal in strong consultation with teachers and parents/caregivers, and they made these goals highly visible (for example, in most classrooms they were hung up in the room, or pasted on windows etc); and

- included multiple *Review/Evaluation* activities including: documentary analysis of student goals; focus groups with parents/caregivers and students; surveys conducted with staff and parents/caregivers; self-review by students, teachers, and herself via the use of GAS at a meta, or overview, level.

The principal, teachers and students alike had goals showing shift in depth and had lift in terms of being stretched to higher goals.

The use of GAS at a meta-level was particularly interesting. Principal A drew directly from the achievement expectations in her deep plan to establish outcomes for the GAS. Because she wanted to focus at the meta-level, she chose as outcome statements:

- Joint goals clearly collaboratively established by all parties (students, their parents/caregivers and teachers);
- Goals regularly revisited, progress checked and feedback provided through a 'shared learning process' between students, their parents/caregivers and teachers;
- Teacher and parent/caregiver reporting of effectiveness of the process, goal monitoring and achievement;
- Students' self-review showing effectiveness of process, goal monitoring and achievement; and
- Principal and teacher self-review showing effectiveness of actions they undertook to support each student in achieving their goal.

Principal A asked all teachers and Governors (46 in total) to rate the achievement of these outcomes using the GAS. I will not include the comprehensive outline of all of the GAS results, but Table 5.1 shows the summarized responses for the first two of her stated outcomes.

As Table 5.1 shows all respondents rated GAS levels for the stated outcomes positively in all categories, though the majority of the respondents scored +1 rather than +2 indicating there was still room for further improvement. The scaling provided Principal A and Board of Governors with a clear summary of the success of goal pursuit in the school and this has subsequently led to Governor support for the further implementation of this FAR Model deep goal pursuit approach for learning.

TABLE 5.1 GAS use at a meta-level in School A

Collation Sheet	Goal Attainment Score					Total
	−2	−1	0	1	2	
Joint Goal Clearly Collaboratively Established—all parties	Teacher makes goal with child—no family/caregiver turns up	Parent only wants teacher input for goal—child in attendance	Parent attends with child but relies on child and teacher for goal setting	Goal collaboratively formed at Student Learning conference	Input prior—thought and feedback informs draft goal and all parties involved in final goal establishment	
	5	0	1	23	17	46
Goal regularly revisited, progress checked and feedback provided through Shared Learning process	−2	−1	0	1	2	Total
	Teacher feedback only	Some feedback not related to goal, negative	Feedback related to goal	Intermittent feedback to child about goal	Regular feedback/feed forward to child from parent and teacher specific to goal	
	2	0	3	29	12	46

Principal A also employed an independent evaluator to gather feedback from students, Governors and teachers on the effectiveness of the goal focus in the school. A selection of some of the student feedback illustrates the impact. Two junior students (under nine years) noted generally about focusing on goals: "*they* [having clear goals] *helped with learning*"; and "*made me think about what I was doing*". Several students in this younger group, in varied ways, referred to advantages in the home and school learning link with two reporting: "*They* [parents/caregivers] *know what's best for you at school*"; and "*Goals were helpful because you can work on them at home and at school*". One student stated that when the goals were on the wall they remembered them, but when they were taken down they forgot them. The senior students (9–12 years) reiterated the same points about focusing learning and thinking, and home and school partnership, but several of these older students were clear that if the goal was too easy they needed to set a new, more challenging, goal. When such goals were chosen, as one student noted: "*I had to work hard to achieve the goal*".

Overall the feedback provided by all of the stakeholders can be summarized in the following key points:

- Goal setting enhanced and focused learning and thinking;
- Joint goal setting with parents/caregivers, students and teachers created a bridge to home and extended learning;
- Full commitment was needed from all three partners for goal achievement;
- Ongoing visibility/accessibility of goals was important for refocusing;
- Goal achievement was associated with hard work; and
- Easy goals provided little challenge.

In the 'Reporting' phase of the project in School A the principal ensured sharing of all results from this meta-level activity with stakeholders. She held meetings with staff, Governors and parents-caregivers at which she presented a final report that included an overview of the project, meta-level phase findings, and recommendations for further improvement. She also included a summary of this material in the parent/caregiver regular newsletter and her annual report to the Board of Governors. Further, because the meta-level activity was in fact a personal performance review goal, Principal A comprehensively outlined all plans and evidence at her annual performance review meeting. An interesting outcome of the reporting has been the wider dissemination of the outcomes of this goal pursuit project within the education sector.

Principal A has been invited to share an outline of the process and outcomes of this meta-level goal pursuit at multiple principal association meetings. The project represents a rare example of application of focused goal pursuit that has relevance to both the performance review and student learning contexts and has generated considerable interest from others in the sector.

> Think about a meta-level goal pursuit possibility within your own context.
>
> ▸ What would be the focus of your goal pursuit?
>
> ▸ What detailed elements of the FAR Model phases would you include?
>
> ▸ Who would you involve as key collaborative colleagues in this pursuit and how would you engage them?

How the meta-level case stacked up against the research and neuroleadership thinking

The meta-level improvement initiative embarked upon at School A can be examined against a range of elements of effectiveness suggested by key authors in the field of goal pursuit, all of whom are noted earlier in this book. As the following account shows, goal pursuit in School A strongly matched the elements of effectiveness reported by multiple researchers.

Research match

As outlined in the earlier description of the FAR Model phases undertaken at School A, the principal worked deliberately to ensure there was a shared sense of purpose and direction, and conditions were established to enable others to be effective (Leithwood & Reihl, 2003). These two Preparatory phase activities were evidenced in my observation of all stakeholders having strong commitment to the goal pursuit resulting from extensive communication, dialogue and support. Principal A facilitated multiple professional development sessions to engage teachers in learning about goal pursuit and how to use this to focus student learning. She allocated funding for time release for staff for the development as well as providing meeting expenses for later caregiver interactions that were necessary. She relentlessly mentored staff in their work with students.

The School A initiative also met most of Latham and Locke's (2003) expansion upon what is required from leadership and teachers to ensure success in goal pursuit. There was, from my observation:

- a clear target and timeframe for the goal;
- somewhat of a match between level of difficulty of the goal and the self-confidence of those involved, though with the students this confidence grew with time;
- opportunity to learn how to link data to the action steps;
- strong collaboration in every phase;
- knowledge about curriculum etc so that appropriate goals for students were set;
- commitment made publicly about the goal;
- linkage made between the goal and the bigger picture direction for learning;
- demonstrated commitment to the goal by Principal A's attendance at development, meetings etc. on goal pursuit;
- involvement of all stakeholders in goal pursuit with students;
- continual feedback on goal progress and achievement at both student and meta-level; and
- provision of implementation support.

At School A there was also an overt demonstration of the elements of effectiveness identified by Kouzes and Posner (2007) who suggest that leaders should hold high and clear expectations and goals, create conditions for success, provide good feedback around goal achievement, personalize recognition and feedback, incentivize, thank and be thoughtful. Further, at School A, there was an alignment with conditions suggested by Goleman, Byzatis and McKee (2004) for goals: built on strength, not weaknesses; developed by the student (or if a staff goal, the teacher), not someone else; which were feasible and had manageable steps; and somewhat matched the person's learning style.

...goal pursuit in School A strongly matched the elements of effectiveness reported by multiple researchers.

Neuroleadership match

The School A example also indicates application of current thinking about goal pursuit in the neuroleadership arena that is referred to in detail in Chapter 2. If using the SCARF model from neuroleadership as a touchstone for checking how well the initiative stacked up, the use of public display and recognition of goals enhanced the 'Status' element. Goal setting and achievement itself had the intent of enhancing 'Certainty' and the FAR Model itself has strong planning and phased activity elements. The responsibility for establishing the plan and phases for goal pursuit was controlled primarily by the person who set the goal, whether that was Principal A, a teacher, or student: a focus on the 'Autonomy' element was therefore high. The authentic collaboration approach deliberately modelled by the principal and then mirrored in teacher, parent/caregiver and student interactions matched the 'Relatedness' feature in the SCARF model. Both 'Relatedness' and 'Fairness' were evidenced in non-defensive, transparent, open interactions, and clarity around expectations for achievement.

In terms of Berkman and Rock's (2012) AIM model, all 'Antecedents' for achieving goals were present in terms of: 'Stickiness' (the goals were visible—student goals were hanging up in all classrooms and therefore tangible, memorable); 'Motivation' (gain-framed goals were set for the Principal herself, teachers and students and enhanced the chance of longer-term, more sustainable results); and 'Social context' (the students engaged in dialogue about their goals with caregivers and teachers and teachers engaged in dialogue about their goals together, with their team leader, and with Principal A). 'Integration' (ongoing goal pursuit) was shown particularly with Principal A and teachers who had 'why' and 'how' elements incorporated within goal deep plans. 'Managing rewards and anticipation' (goal habit formation) also occurred with the steps in the FAR Model deep action plans making achievement visible, the sharing of success (in small step victory style) continuously encouraged in varied dialogue settings, and the rewards made explicit in GAS. A summary of a strong match between the School A goal pursuit and the neuroleadership elements is shown in Table 5.2.

TABLE 5.2 School A goal pursuit match to key neuroleadership elements

Neuroleadership Element	Match in School A Goal Pursuit
Status (goals should create learning and improvement; positive feedback given)	Public display and recognition of goals.
Certainty (clear planning; incremental steps)	Goal setting and achievement itself was a demonstration of certainty. FAR Model had clear planning and steps.
Autonomy (goal pursuer in the driver seat; ownership, not imposition of goals)	Establishing the plan and phases for goal pursuit was controlled primarily by the person who set the goal.
Relatedness (Collaborative, supportive, sharing ethos; lowering of defensiveness and enhancing dialogue)	Approach modelled by Principal A and then mirrored in teacher, parent/caregiver and student interactions matched authentic collaboration and lowered defensiveness.
Fairness (increasing transparency, openness; clarity around expectations of achievement)	Both 'Relatedness' and 'Fairness' were evidenced in non-defensive, transparent, and open interactions as well as planning.
Antecedents (stickiness, motivation, social context)	Goals were visible—student goals were hanging up in all classrooms and therefore tangible, memorable). Gain-framed goals were set for the Principal herself, teachers and students. Students, caregivers, teachers, team leaders and Principal A all engaged in dialogue about goals.
Integration (ongoing goal pursuit)	Shown where Principal A and teachers had 'why' and 'how' elements incorporated within goal deep plans.
Managing Rewards and Anticipation (goal habit formation)	Occurred with the steps in the FAR Model deep action plans making achievement visible, the sharing of success continuously encouraged in varied dialogue settings, and the rewards made explicit in GAS.

The School A example therefore stacks up well as an example of application of goal pursuit. This is a rare example because despite the fact that schools have talked about goals and goal achievement for decades, there is limited research on the depth of goal setting or the leadership of it at the school-wide level referred to in this case study.

Summary

- Goal pursuit in School A followed all underpinning principles and phases of the FAR Model.
- Principal A had this project as the focus of her performance review so cascading and alignment of goals was evident.
- Goal pursuit in this school is considered as meta-level because a school-wide goal was set for the topic of improving goal pursuit itself within the whole school.
- Meta-level evaluation using survey, focus groups, interviews, documentary analysis and GAS revealed clear improvement and impact, though also highlighting areas for further improvement.
- The FAR Model activity engaged in for this meta-level project in School A matched current thinking and research associated with goal setting and achievement.
- The activity also strongly matched neuroleadership elements of the SCARF and AIM models.

6
Ten Useful Activities, Tools and Templates

Abstract: *Chapter 6 includes multiple activities, tools and templates for the approach to goal pursuit outlined in the book with sequencing of activities to match the phases in the FAR Model. Each activity or tool has been employed successfully and I hope they will be easy to download and implement in any education context.*

Keywords: templates for goal pursuit; tools

Piggot-Irvine, Eileen. *Goal Pursuit in Education Using Focused Action Research*. New York: Palgrave Macmillan, 2015. DOI: 10.1057/9781137505125.0011.

Introduction

This final chapter of the book includes an array of activity ideas (reflection and implementation tools and templates) for a goal pursuit project which you might embark upon for yourself, team or organization. Many of the activities have been used previously in the book when describing application.

I hope you find these tools and templates a useful starting point in developing an authentically collaborative goal pursuit approach which has alignment of goals between individual, team, the organization, and perhaps regional or national initiatives. I also hope the activities assist you in creating shift in depth and specificity, and lift in challenge.

I have sequenced activity ideas in this chapter to follow a progression in the FAR Model for goal pursuit. You might consider these as activities with stakeholders involved in any specific goal pursuit. The activities progress from Preparatory (clarifying principles for goal pursuit for your organization, aligning and cascading goals) to Reconnaissance phase (becoming 'informed', collecting data on the current situation) to Implementation phase planning (developing deep action plans) to Evaluation phase (collecting data on achievement) and then developing Recommendations and Reporting.

Activity 1: clarifying principles for goal pursuit for your organization

This Preparatory phase activity is designed to both assist in clarifying which of the principles for goal pursuit are important to your organization and to enhance engagement and ownership of key people (those most likely to influence or be impacted by the goals) from the very outset.

With a group of key stakeholders in your organization, brainstorm the leadership and implementation principles underpinning an approach to goal pursuit for your organization. Draw upon the research, theory and any other material offered in this book to help distil the principles.

Record in Table 6.1 the principles for both:

- leading the process; and
- implementing goal pursuit by others such as staff etc.

I have shown an example to get you started in each column.

TABLE 6.1 *Principles underpinning leading and implementation of goal pursuit*

Leadership Principles	Implementation Principles
– alignment and cascading assured	– insert a Governance Board meeting agenda item to determine which strategic goals will align with the national or regional goals
– authentic collaboration principles adopted	– decide which principles are important for our organization and develop a protocol for use

Activity 2: aligning, cascading, goals in Preparatory phase

This activity can also be used in the Preparatory phase of the FAR Model for goal pursuit. Cascading of goals from a national or regional level through to the organization, team and individual is important if alignment is to occur.

Complete each layer of the cascading circles in Figure 6.1 by filling in a national or regional priority which is important to your organization. If there is no necessity in your organization to align with national or regional goals, then move to the organization strategic goal circle as the starting point. Incrementally work inward to the individual goal(s) by recording goals that align, have clear links, to this national or regional goal.

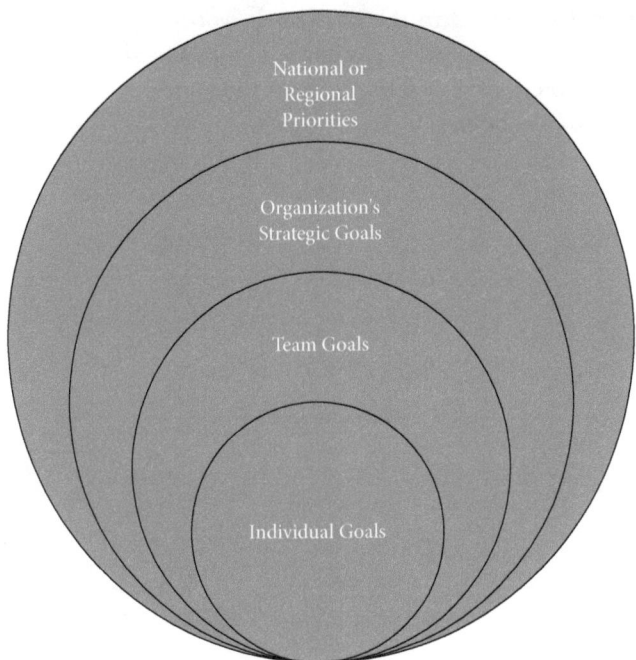

FIGURE 6.1   *Cascading goals for your own organization*

Activity 3: brainstorming 'literature review' ideas to become 'informed' in the Reconnaissance phase

In the Reconnaissance phase of the FAR Model for goal pursuit an initial activity is to become 'informed' about what is considered to be 'effective' by previous authors and researchers who have written about the focus of your chosen goal. Remember, if this is a team or organization goal, the activity of becoming informed should be conducted with other key people who are influenced or may be impacted by the goal. Such collaboration will enhance their 'buy-in' to the goal pursuit. Ideally, you would meet with these people to brainstorm the topics of importance when recording information from articles, how you will share the reading/articles to summarize the important features of effectiveness, and then re-meet to further distil the summaries. Figure 6.2 outlines an approach for recording initial brainstorming topics for what could be described here as a 'mini literature review'.

In Figure 6.2 brainstorm the key search words and phrases you will use to find previous research, readings, documents and other information relevant to effective practice in your topic area. Add any resources you already know about.

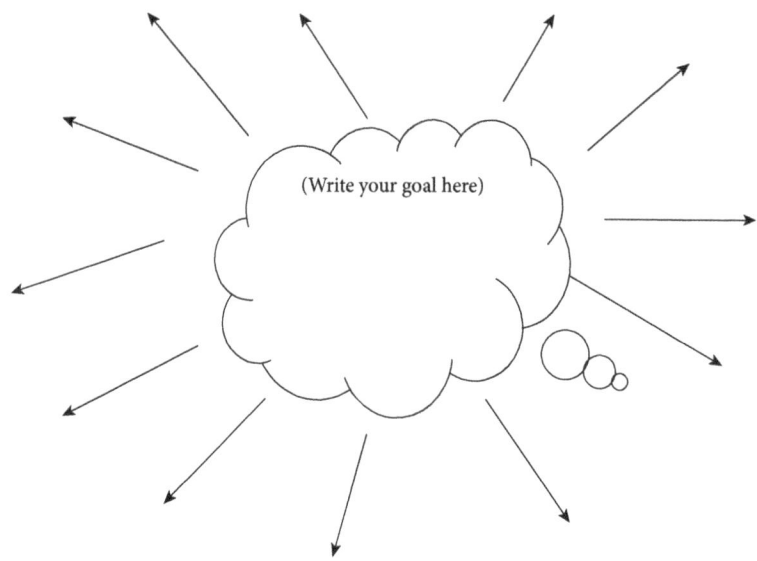

FIGURE 6.2   *Brainstorming literature review topics*

TABLE 6.2   *Locating key literature or other reference sources*

Topic Literature, Relevant Resources	Location
Authentic collaboration	Argyris and Schön (1996); Piggot-Irvine (2012); Senge et al. (2000)

Activity 4: planning for collecting data for Reconnaissance phase in the FAR Model

Once again, work collaboratively with your key stakeholders to decide and plan for how you might gather data about the existing situation associated with your goal focus. List possible data collection methods in Table 6.3. Remember to think 'manageable, realistic and achievable'.

TABLE 6.3 *Data collection for Reconnaissance phase*

	What is the method?	Who will be asked or what will be investigated?	If asking, how many people will be asked?	How will these people be selected?	What will be asked or examined?
Method 1					
Method 2					

Activity 5: summarizing findings from the Reconnaissance phase in the FAR Model

Before moving to the Implementation phase in the FAR Model for goal pursuit there is a need to distil, analyse, summarize and record the important findings from the Reconnaissance phase. You may not need guidance, or a format, for progressively recording this summarizing, but if you do you might find Table 6.4 helpful.

TABLE 6.4 *Analysis and reflection upon the Reconnaissance results*

What are the main points from the literature review?

What are your main findings from the Reconnaissance phase data-gathering?

What do these two sets of information suggest to you needs to be improved?

Of these ideas for improvement, what are the most important/urgent/interesting/relevant things? (a maximum of say three only)

Activity 6: planning for the Implementation phase in the FAR Model

The data collected in the Reconnaissance phase of the FAR Model guides decision making (again collaboratively) about what is to be improved upon in the Implementation phase. More often than not I have experienced that people have wanted to write a full action plan at this point in order to summarize all activity in the goal pursuit. I do not think it matters whether you write a full plan or just focus on the Implementation phase but I encourage most often the full plan approach because it provides such a good overview as a summary. The two plan outlines I am including here offer the opportunity for a full plan, but it is your choice to decide if it is a single phase that you want to extract.

Write your own personal FAR Model type deep goal pursuit plan for a specific goal you have in mind.

Remember, if you are a leader, your role may be more like that of Principal A, i.e. showing you are leading others in goal pursuit! If this is the case you might be focused on: bringing yourself up to speed on what goal pursuit involves; engaging other staff and other key stakeholders (those influencing and impacted) in order to gain 'buy-in'; providing development to ensure staff in leadership positions are prepared for the task of working with other team members; providing ongoing support and resources to ensure the implementation will succeed; planning for both formative and summative review of the initiative; disseminating review findings; and planning for sustaining the initiative.

I am providing two options as templates for drawing up the deep plan as Tables 6.5 and Table 6.6.

TABLE 6.5   Deep level plan: Template 1

Goal	Actions	Measurable Outcomes	Resources/s (Recorded for each action)	Date for Completion
To	*Reconnaissance Phase*			
	Becoming Informed 1. Do some reading on .... and develop criteria for effectiveness	Knowledge of effective............, and a clear set of criteria for this	1.	....
	Current Situation Analysis) 2. Check how I .... currently against the criteria by: a.	A summary of findings from data collection.....	2. a	....
	b.		2. b	
	Planning for Improvement 3. Think about the results for 2 and develop a plan for the way I will improve	Implementation plan developed	3. Nil	
	Carrying out Plan 4.	Record/log reflections on achievement	4.	....
	5.		5.	....
	6.		6.	
	Evaluation 7. Collect data on improvements	Improvement shown as recorded in	7.	....
	8. Report findings to .... and engage in dialogue to get response to findings on achievement as well as ideas for further improvement	8. Findings and ideas for further improvement written up and reported to key stakeholders in a way which opens up dialogue.	8.	....

TABLE 6.6 *Deep level plan: Template 2*

Objective	Actions	Measurable Outcomes	Date for Completion	Self-Review
To …..	*Reconnaissance* 1. 2. 3. *Planning for Implementation* 4. *Carrying out Implementation* 5. *Evaluation* 6. Formative 7. Summative *Reporting*			

Activity 7: evaluation of Implementation phase activity

In the Evaluation phase of the FAR Model for goal pursuit once again there is activity associated with data collection in order to provide evidence for achievement of the actions noted in the Implementation phase. Table 6.7 might provide you with a guide to planning for this data collection. Note that this activity specifically outlines one potential evaluation method i.e. a GAS template. You will have read earlier in Chapter 5 that Principal A employed a number of evaluation methods including surveys, focus groups, documentary analysis of goals and achievement outcomes, as well as GAS.

List possible data collection methods and associated key guiding elements. Remember to think about keeping this manageable, realistic and achievable.

TABLE 6.7 *Planning for Evaluation phase data collection*

Implementation change to be evaluated	What method?	Who will be asked, or what documents will be analysed?	How many people will be asked? Which documents selected?	How will these people and documents be selected?	What will be asked, examined?

Activity 8: GAS as a specific Evaluation phase activity

GAS as an Evaluation phase tool has been given some emphasis in this book. To reiterate, I think this is a powerful tool primarily when employed not only as a self-reflected tool by the goal pursuer but also in dialogue between that person or team and others who can provide feedback. I have also acknowledged earlier how initially complex it looks to set up all of the attainment levels, but once established you should see there is a fairly simple pattern involving transposing the outcomes directly from the FAR Model deep plan followed by identification of each attainment level. The latter are really quite easy to determine!

Use the template in Table 6.8 to create a GAS that would allow you to rate the success of your plan developed in Activity 6.

TABLE 6.8 *GAS for use with your own deep plan*

Outcome Attainment Levels	Reconnaissance Outcome 1	Reconnaissance Outcome 2	Implementation Outcome	Evaluation Outcome 1	Expected Outcome 2
Most unfavourable outcomes (−2)					
Less than expected success with outcomes (−1)					
Expected level outcomes (0)					
More than expected success with outcomes (+1)					
Best anticipated success with outcomes (+2)					
Comments:					

Activity 9: ensuring ownership of the findings and recommendations through FFA

Gaining ownership of findings and recommendations and 'buy-in' for further improvement based on those findings is most important if sustained improvement is to be an outcome of goal pursuit. Earlier I have plugged strongly for the use of Force Field Analysis (FFA) as an activity to achieve this important engagement of others. In Chapter 3, an overview has been provided for this tool as well as provision of a generic FFA graphic. Here, I am including as Table 6.9 a step-by-step process outline that I developed recently. The outline is prefaced by whole group prioritizing of the most important recommendations to be implemented. The outline shows suggested timings for each step because as a facilitator of this activity I have found that it is important to have a degree of time pressure around the steps.

TABLE 6.9 *FFA process steps*

1. Select: a facilitator, a timekeeper, and a presenter for each group of approx. eight people (2 mins)
2. Discuss and then write the desired outcome (or could be stated as 'ideal solution') at the top of chart paper e.g. *All staff have a clear understanding of the principles of effective goal pursuit and we develop a process outline that matches the principles* (5 mins)
3. Brainstorm (on scrap paper) all factors that will lead towards the desired outcome (Drivers) (10 mins)
4. Brainstorm all factors that will detract from the desired outcome (Resistors) (10 mins)
5. Allocate relative weightings to each factor (e.g., 1=low importance to 5=high importance) (10 mins)
6. Draw arrows for each driving force factor (arrow size = relative weighting)
7. Draw arrows for each resisting force factor (5 mins for 6 & 7)
8. Identify the two most significant driving force as well as resisting force factors (5 mins)
9. Brainstorm strategies to strengthen the two significant driving force factors and reduce, minimize, the two resisting force factors (15 mins—you might want to split your group to do this)
10. Convert these strategies to an action plan (to be presented to whole group) detailing each strategy implementation (15 mins).

Activity 10: reflecting on Evaluation phase findings and Reporting

The FAR Model does not actually imply a 'final' phase of activity. In my experience there are always ongoing activities, further ideas for improvement, as well as recommendations resulting from the Evaluation phase. First, Table 6.10 provides an outline for how you might record information about findings from the Evaluation phase, conclusions and recommendations. Second, Table 6.11 provides a guide to what you might consider in a final report for the overall goal pursuit project.

TABLE 6.10 *Reflecting and reporting on results*

What subheadings could you use to organize your Evaluation phase reporting?
What are your main findings from the Evaluation phase data-gathering?
What conclusions can you draw from the findings?
What recommendations can be implied from the conclusions?

Your report could be considered as a 'case study' of your goal pursuit project. There are many ways you could write this and your own organization might have its own format. Often reporting is organized under the headings shown in Table 6.11.

TABLE 6.11 *Final report writing outline for overall project*

Introduction	• Description of your organization • Description of your goal pursuit team • Brief rationale for your goal selection • Key phases overview diagram for your goal pursuit
Reconnaissance phase	Key Activities and Outcomes
Implementation phase	Key Activities and Outcomes
Evaluation phase	Key Activities and Outcomes
Conclusion and Recommendations	• Conclusions • Recommendations
• References • Appended data-gathering tools • Appended important documents	

References

Altrichter, H., Kemmis, S., McTaggart, R., & Zuber-Skerritt, O. (2000). The concept of action research. *The Learning Organisation, 9*(3), 125–131.

Appelbaum, S. H., & Wohl, L. (2000). Transformation or change: Some prescriptions for health care organizations. *Managing Service Quality, 10*(5), 279–298. doi:10.1108/09604520010345768.

Argyris, C. (2003). A life full of learning. *Organization Studies, 24*, 1178–1192.

Argyris, C., & Schön, D. A. (1974). *Theory in practice: Increasing professional effectiveness.* San Francisco, CA: Jossey Bass.

Argyris, C., & Schön, D. A. (1996). *Organizational learning 11: Theory, method and practice.* Reading, MA: Addison Wesley.

Asplund, J., & Blacksmith, N. (2013). *Strength-based goal setting.* Retrieved 1 October 2013, from Gallup Business Journal: http://businessjournal.gallup.com/content/152981/strengths-based-goal-setting.aspx.

Berkman, E., & Rock, D. (2012). Focus your AIM: A social cognitive neuroscience model for goal pursuit. 2012 Neuroleadership Summit Highlights. http://blog.neuroleadership.org/2012_11_01_archive.html.

Bovend'Eerdt, T. J. H., Botell, R. E., & Wade, D. T. (2009). Writing SMART rehabilitation goals and achieving goal attainment scaling: A practical guide. *Clinical Rehabilitation, 23*, 352–361.

Brooker, R., & Macpherson, I. (1999). Communicating the processes and outcomes of practitioner research:

An opportunity for self-indulgence or a serious professional responsibility. *Educational Action Research*, 7(2), 207–221.

Bushe, G. R., & Marshak, R. J. (2009). Revisioning organization development: Diagnostic and dialogic premises and patterns of practice. *Journal of Applied Behavioral Science, 45*, 348–368. doi:10.1177/0021886309335070.

Busher, H., & Harris, A. (2000). *Subject leadership and school improvement*. London: Paul Chapman Publishing.

Cacioppo, J. T., & Patrick, B. (2008). *Loneliness: Human nature and the need for social connection*. New York: W.W. Norton and Company.

Cardno, C. (2001). Managing dilemmas in appraising performance: An approach for school leaders. In D. Middlewood & C. Cardno (Eds.), *Managing teacher appraisal and performance: A comparative approach* (pp. 143–159). London: Routledge Falmer.

Cardno, C. (2003). *Action research: A developmental approach*. Wellington: New Zealand Council for Educational Research.

Cardno, C., & Piggot-Irvine, E. (1996). Incorporating action research in school senior management training. *The International Journal of Educational Management, 10*(5), 19–24.

Coghlan, D., & Brannick, T. (2010). *Doing action research in your own organisation*. Thousand Oaks, CA: Sage.

Cohen, L., Manion, L., & Morrison, K. (2007). *Research methods in education* (6th ed.). London: Routledge.

Conzemius, A., & O'Neill, J. (2006). *Building shared responsibility for student learning*. Alexandria: Association for Supervision and Curriculum Development.

Creswell, J. W., & Plano Clark, V. L. (2011). *Designing and conducting mixed methods research* (2nd ed.). Thousand Oaks: Sage Publications.

Cummings, T. C. & Worely, C. G. (2009). *Organization development and change*. Ohio: South-Western Cengage Learning.

Dick, B. (2004). Action research literature: Themes and trends. *Action Research On-Line, 2*, 425–444.

Eisenberger, N. I., Lieberman, M. D., & Williams, K. D. (2003). Does rejection hurt? An fMRI study of social exclusion. *Science, 302*, 290–292.

Erez, M., Earley, P. C., & Hulin, C. L. (1985). The impact of participation on goal acceptance and performance: A two-step model. *Academy of Management Journal, 28*(1), 50–66. Retrieved from http://www.jstor.org/pss/256061.

Ferguson, M. J., & Porter, S. C. (2010). What is implicit about goal pursuit? In B. Gawronski & K. Payne (Eds.), *Handbook of Implicit Social Cognition: Measurement, Theory, and Applications*, (pp. 311–334). New York: Guilford Press.

Goleman, D., Byatzis, R., & McKee, A. (2004). *Primal leadership: Learning to lead with emotional intelligence.* Boston: Harvard Business School Press.

Gordon, G. (2006). *Building engaged schools: Getting the most out of American classrooms.* New York: Gallup.

Gordon, E. (2013). Neuroleadership and integrative neuroscience: It's about validation, stupid! In D. Rock & A. Ringleb, *Handbook of NeuroLeadership*, (pp. 95–125). New York: NeuroLeadership Institute.

Hattori, R. A., & Lapidus, T. (2004). Collaboration, trust and innovative change. *Journal of Change Management*, 4(2), 97–104.

Institute for Education Leadership, IEL, (2011). Exploring five core leadership capacities. Setting goals: The power of purpose. *Ontario Leadership Strategy Bulletin #4*, Winter 2010/11. www.ontario.ca/leadership.

Johnson, R. B., & Onwuegbuzie, A. J. (2004). Mixed methods research: A research paradigm whose time has come. *Educational Researcher*, 33(7), 14–26.

Kaplan, R. S., & Norton, D. P. (2001). *The strategy-focused organization.* Boston: Harvard Business School Press.

Kouzes, J. M., & Posner, B. Z. (2007). *The leadership challenge.* San Francisco: Jossey-Bass.

Lafferty, C. L., & Alford, K. L. (2010). NeuroLeadership: Sustaining research relevance into the 21st Century. *S.A.M. Advanced Management Journal*, Summer, 32–42.

Latham, G. P. (2004). The motivation benefits of goal setting. *Academy of Management Executive*, 18(4), 126–129.

Latham, G. P., & Locke, E. A. (2006). Enhancing the benefits and overcoming the pitfalls of goal setting. *Organizational Dynamics*, 35(4), 332–340.

Leithwood, K., & Reihl, C. (2003). *What we know about successful school leadership.* Philadelphia: Laboratory for Student Success, Temple University.

Leithwood, K., Aitken, R. & Jantzi, D. (2006). *Making schools smarter: Leading with evidence.* Thousand Oaks: Corwin Press.

Locke, E. A. (1968). Toward a theory of task motivation and incentives. *Organizational Behaviour and Human Performance,* 3(2), 157–189.

Locke, E. A., & Latham, G. P. (2002). Building a practically useful theory of goal setting and task motivation: A 35-year odyssey. *American Psychologist,* 57(9), 705–717.

Locke, E. A., & Latham, G. P. (2006). New directions in goal-setting theory. *Current Directions in Psychological Science,* 15(5), 265–268. doi: 10.1111/j.1467-8721.2006.00449.

Locke, E. A., & Latham, G. P. (2013). *New developments in goal setting and task performance.* New York: Routledge.

Louie, K., & Glimcher, P. W. (2012). Efficient coding and the neural representation of value. *Annals of the New York Academy of Sciences,* 1251, 13–32. Issue: The Year in Cognitive Neuroscience. doi: 10.1111/j.1749-6632.2012.06496.x.

McKay, J., & Kember, D. (1997). Spoon feeding leads to regurgitation: A better diet can result in more digestible learning outcomes. *Higher Education Research & Development,* 16(1), 55–67.

McMorland, J., & Piggot-Irvine, E. (2000). Facilitation as midwifery: Facilitation and praxis in group learning. *Systematic Practice and Action,* 13(2), 121–127.

McNiff, J. (1988). *Action research: Principles and practice.* Hampshire: McMillan Education Ltd.

McTaggart, R. (1991). *Action research: A short modern history.* Geelong, Australia: Deakin University Press.

MacKeracher, D. (2004). *Making sense of adult learning.* Toronto: University of Toronto Press.

Mento, A. J., Steel, R. P., & Karren, R. J. (1987). A meta-analytic study of the effects of goal setting on task performance: 1966–1984. *Organizational Behavior and Human Decision Processes,* 39(1). 52–83.

Miller, G. (2008). Growing pains for fMRI. *SCIENCE,* 320, 1412–1414. www.sciencemag.org.

Mobbs, D., & McFarland, W. (2013). The neuroscience of motivation. In D. Rock & A. Ringleb, *Handbook of NeuroLeadership,* (pp. 491–506). New York: NeuroLeadership Institute.

Molyneux, C., Koo, N., Piggot-Irvine, E., Talmage, A., Travaglia, R., & Willis, M. (2012). Doing it together – collaborative research on goal-setting and review in a music therapy centre. *New Zealand Journal of Music Therapy,* 10, 6–38.

References

Ordóñez, L., Schweitzer, M., Galinsky, A., & Bazerman, M. (2009). Goals gone wild: The systematic side effects of over-prescribing goal setting. *HBS Working Paper*, 09–083. Retrieved 1 October 2013, from http://opimweb.wharton.upenn.edu/documents/research/Goals_Gone_Wild.pdf.

Ospina, S., Dodge, J., Godsoe, B., Minieri, J., Salvador, R., & Schall, E. (2002). From consent to mutual inquiry: Balancing democracy and authority in action research. *Action research*, 2(1), March 2004, 47–69. doi: 10.1177/1476750304040494.

Piggot-Irvine, E. (2012). Creating authentic collaboration: A central feature of effectiveness. In O. Zuber-Skerritt, *Action research for sustainable development in a turbulent world* (pp. 89–107). Bingley, UK: Emerald.

Piggot-Irvine, E. (2010). Confronting evaluation blindness: Evidence of influence of action science based feedback. *American Journal of Evaluation*, 31(3), 314–325, doi: 10.1177/1098214010369251.

Piggot-Irvine, E. (2009). *Action research in practice*. Wellington: NZCER.

Piggot-Irvine, E. (2003). Key features of effective appraisal. *The International Journal of Educational Management*, 17(4), 170–178.

Piggot-Irvine, E. (1996). The introduction of draft national guidelines for performance management in schools in New Zealand. *International Directions in Education*, p. 2.

Piggot-Irvine, E., Connelly, D., Curry, R., Hanna, J., Moodie, M., Palmer, M., Peri, D., & Thompson, A., (2011). Building leadership capacity – sustainable leadership. *Action Research Action Learning Association (ALARA) Monograph Series*, 2, 1–40.

Piggot-Irvine, E., & Doyle, L. (2010). Organizational learning 'in use'. *Journal of Educational Leadership and Policy*. 25(2), 55–72.

Piggot-Irvine, E., & Bartlett, B. (2008). *Evaluating action research*. Wellington: NZCER.

Piggot-Irvine, E., & Cardno, C. (2005). *Appraising performance productively: Integrating accountability and development*. Auckland: Eversleigh Publishing.

Preskill, H., & Torres, R. (1999). *Evaluative inquiry for learning in organizations*. Thousand Oaks, California: Sage.

Reason, P., & Bradbury, H. (2001). Introduction: Inquiry and participation in search of a world worthy of human aspiration. In P. Reason & H. Bradbury (Eds.) *Handbook of action research* (pp. 1–14). Thousand Oaks: CA: Sage.

Ringleb, A, H., & Rock, D. (2013). The emerging field of leadership. In D. Rock & A. Ringleb, *Handbook of NeuroLeadership*, (pp. 4–29). New York: NeuroLeadership Institute.

Roach, A. T., & Elliott, S. N. (2005). Goal attainment scaling: An efficient and effective approach to monitoring student progress. *Teaching Exceptional Children, 37*(4), 8–17.

Robinson, V., Hohepa, M., & Lloyd, C. (2009). School leadership and student outcomes: Identifying what works and why - Best evidence synthesis iteration (BES). New Zealand: Ministry of Education.

Rock, D. (2008). SCARF: a brain-based model for collaborating with and influencing others. *NeuroLeadership Journal, 1*, 44–52.

Rock, D., & Cox, C. (2013). SCARF in 2012: Updating the social neuroscience of collaborating with others. In D. Rock & A. Ringleb, *Handbook of NeuroLeadership*, (pp. 329–350). New York: NeuroLeadership Institute.

Rock, D., Siegel, D. J., Poelmans, S.A.Y., & Payne, J. (2012). The healthy mind platter. *NeuroLeadership Journal, 4*, 40–62.

Sagor, R. (2000). *Guiding school improvement with action research.* Alexandria, VA: Association for Supervision and Curriculum Development (ASCD).

Schön, D.A. (1983). *The reflective practitioner: How professionals think in action.* New York, NY: Basic Books.

Senge, P., Cambron-McCabe, N., Lucas, T., Smith, B., Dutton, J., & Kleiner, A. (2000). A primer to the five disciplines. In *Schools that learn* (pp. 59–98). New York: Doubleday.

Sheldon, K. M. (2002). The self-concordance model of healthy goal striving: When personal goals correctly represent the person. In E. L. Deci, & R. M. Ryan, *Handbook of self-determination research*, (pp. 65–86). New York: University of Rochester Press.

Schultz, W. (1999). The reward signal of midbrain dopamine neurons. *News in Physiological Sciences, 14*(6), 249–255.

Schwering, R. E. (2003). Focusing leadership through force field analysis: New variations on a venerable planning tool. *Leadership & Organization Development Journal, 24*(7), 361–370.

Simons, D. J., & Chabris, C. F. (1999). Gorillas in our midst: Sustained inattentional blindness for dynamic events. *Perception, 28*(9), 1059–1074.

Sitkin, S. B., See, K. E., Miller, C. C., Lawless, M. W., & Carton, A. M. (2011). The paradox of stretch goals: organizations in pursuit of the seemingly impossible. *Academy of Management Review, 36*(3), 544–566.

Snyder, C. R., & Lopez, S. J. (2005) *Handbook of positive psychology.* Oxford.

Sorrentino, D. M. (2006). The seek mentoring program: An application of the goal-setting theory. *Journal of College Student Retention, 8*(2), 241–250.

Street, C. (2010). Application of neuroscience in executive team coaching: The WSR Case. *NeuroLeadership Journal, 3,* 64–77. http://www.humancapitalinitiative.com/files/App-of-NS-in-Executive-Team-Coaching_US.pdf.

Stringer, E. T. (2007). *Action research* (3rd ed.). Thousand Oaks, CA: Sage Publications.

Swann, J. (2013). The rise of objectives and targets – or the end of civilisation as we know it. *Higher Education Review, 45*(2), 41–60.

Tubbs, M. E. (1986). Goal-Setting: A meta-analytic examination of the empirical evidence. *Journal of Applied Psychology, 71*(3), 474.

Uhl-Bien, M., & Marion, R. (2009). Complexity leadership in bureaucratic forms of organizing: A meso mode. *The Leadership Quarterly, 20,* 631–650.

Vorhauser-Smith, S. (2011). The neuroscience of performance. White Paper, http://dcb9maxnxelio.cloudfront.net/wp-content/uploads/2012/06/Neuroscience-of-Performance-People-at-their-Best.pdf.

Wadsworth, Y. (2011). *Building in research and evaluation: Human inquiry for living systems.* Sydney, Australia: Action Research Press, Hawthorn and Allen & Unwin. ISBN 978 1 74237 540 3.

Weisbord, M. (2012). *Productive workplaces: Dignity, meaning, and community in the 21st century* (3rd ed.). San Francisco, CA: Jossey-Bass.

Whiting, J., Jones, E., Rock, D., & Bendit, X. (2013). Lead change with the brain in mind. In D. Rock & A. Ringleb, *Handbook of NeuroLeadership,* (pp. 549–568). New York: NeuroLeadership Institute.

Winter, R. (1987). Managers, spectators, and citizens: Where does theory come from in action research? *Educational Action Research, 6*(3), 361–376.

Zuber-Skerritt, O. (2012). *Action research for sustainable development in a turbulent world.* Bingley, UK: Emerald.

Index

accountability, 3, 9, 54, 56
action research (AR), 3, 5, 10,
    11, 32, 33, 40, 54, 63, 75
action research and depth,
    7, 8, 12
AIM model in
    neuroleadership, 24, 26,
    29, 36, 60, 66, 85, 87
antecedents in goal pursuit, 24,
    26, 85, 86
authentic collaboration, 3, 6, 9,
    11, 16, 25, 32, 34, 43, 53, 55,
    56, 58, 65, 67, 68, 70, 85, 86
authentic collaboration and
    trust, 75
dialogue and authentic
    collaboration, 73
levels of collaboration, 70
skills for authentic
    collaboration, 71, 73, 74
autonomy in goal pursuit,
    24, 85, 86

becoming informed, 42, 43, 59,
    91, 95
'buy-in', ownership, 8, 53, 54,
    55, 59, 65, 91, 94, 98

cascading of goals, 8, 9, 18, 35,
    36, 37, 39, 77, 87, 90
case study, 11, 66, 75, 76,
    86, 100
certainty in goal pursuit,
    24, 25, 85, 86

challenge, 6, 7, 11, 19, 58, 63
clarifying principles in goal
    pursuit, 5, 89
clear expectations, 17, 26, 84

data-based decision making.
    See evidence
defensive, 8, 11, 25, 68, 69, 70,
    71, 73, 74, 86
depth, 6, 9, 11, 12, 33, 34, 45, 50,
    58, 61, 75, 77, 80, 86, 89
depth example, 58
depth in goal pursuit, 3
developmental, 3, 9, 32, 66, 67
dialogue, 8, 25, 26, 43, 49, 53,
    58, 63, 65, 67, 69, 70, 73,
    74, 75, 84, 85, 86, 95, 98
advocacy, 68, 69, 73, 75
inquiry, 68, 69, 70, 73, 75
double-loop learning, 74, 75

Evaluation phase of action
    research, 5, 6, 9, 11, 12,
    16, 46, 48, 50, 51, 56, 59,
    62, 64, 80, 89, 95, 97, 98,
    100, 101
evidence, 5, 6, 11, 12, 15, 30, 33,
    40, 50, *See* depth
evidence-based
    discussion, 26
defensive response, 68
dialogue, 69, 73, 74
Evaluation phase, 10, 47, 51,
    59, 97

evidence—*Continued*
  evidence of improvement, 50
  lack of/limited evidence, 33, 59
  learning evidence, 47
  productive response,
    68, 69, 73
  performance review, 59, 82
  Reconnaissance phase, 40, 45
evidence in goal pursuit, 3

fairness in goal pursuit, 24, 25, 36,
  85, 86
feedback, 18, 19, 24, 33, 41, 44, 47, 55,
  58, 62, 65, 66, 68, 69, 71, 73, 75, 80,
  81, 84, 86, 98
Focused Action Research Model
  (FAR), 5, 6, 32–56
force field analysis (FFA), 52, 53,
  98, 99
formative, 66, 72, 73, 94

goal attainment scaling (GAS), 10, 11,
  12, 47, 49, 50, 51, 80, 81, 85, 87,
  97, 98
goal definition, 14
goal pursuit definition, 2
goal setting, 3, 9, 14, 17, 18, 19, 37, 39,
  45, 52, 54, 58, 78, 81, 82, 85, 86, 87
governors, 36, 39, 43, 46, 77, 80, 82

Implementation phase in action
  research, 5, 43, 45, 46, 56, 79, 89,
  93, 94, 97
inauthentic collaboration, 67, 68
integration in goal pursuit, 24, 26, 27,
  60, 85, 86

ladder of inference, 74
leaders, 8, 9, 17, 36, 37, 39, 42, 43, 46, 47,
  51, 56, 84, 86
learning objectives, 15, 30
literature review, 41, 78, 91, 92, 93

maintenance in goal pursuit, 24, 27
meta-level goal pursuit, 77, 80, 81, 82, 87

motivation, 14, 17, 27, 30, 36, 61, 66, 75,
  78, 85, 86

neuroleadership, 5, 10, 11, 20, 30, 36, 42,
  60, 61, 66, 83, 85, 87
  approach conditions, 21, 22, 23, 24,
    25, 30, 66
  avoid conditions, 23, 25
neuroscience, 5, 10, 11, 14, 20, 28
non-defensive, 26, 43, 68, 70, 71, 75, 85,
  86, *See* productive
non-education sector, 17, 18, 19, 20,
  35, 37

organizational goals, 14, 18

parents, 37, 41, 43, 46, 49, 77, 80, 82
performance review, 3, 8, 9, 12, 37, 39,
  58, 59, 61, 66, 77, 82, 83, 87
performance review and authentic
  collaboration, 9
planning, 6, 25, 43, 44, 46, 52, 54, 59,
  62, 79, 85, 86, 89, 94, 95, 96
  depth in planning, 33, 46, 51,
    60, 64
  strategic planning, 8
prefrontal cortex (PFC), 21, 23, 25, 30
  stress impact, 22
Preparatory phase of action research,
  5, 15, 18, 34, 38, 39, 65, 83, 89, 90
productive, 11, 68, 70
professional development, 39, 78, 84

rationale for goals, 14
Recommendations phase of action
  research, 5, 6, 12, 46, 52, 54, 55, 56,
  82, 89, 98, 100
Reconnaissance phase of action
  research, 5, 6, 15, 16, 39, 41,
  42, 43, 44, 46, 47, 56, 78, 89, 91, 93,
  94, 95
reflecting-in-action, 74
reflections, 6, 44, 50, 95
relatedness in goal pursuit, 24, 25, 27,
  66, 85, 86

DOI: 10.1057/9781137505125.0013

Reporting phase of action research, 5, 6, 12, 33, 52, 54, 55, 56, 65, 83, 100
SCARF model in neuroleadership, 24, 27, 29, 36, 42, 66, 85, 87
selecting goals, 5, 15, 18, 36
self-efficacy, 14, 19
self-regulation, 14
sharing goals, 19, 25, 27, 36, 52, 54, 55, 59, 66, 82, 85, 86
SMART goals, 20, 26
social context, 27, 36, 66, 85, 86
status in goal pursuit, 24, 86
students and goal pursuit, 10, 15, 30, 36, 39, 46, 49, 77, 80, 82, 84, 85, 86
summative, 66, 72, 94
surface approach, 58, 59, 64

teachers, 17, 39, 41, 43, 44, 45, 47, 49, 77, 80, 82, 84, 85, 86
tools for goal pursuit, 4, 12, 17, 47, 54, 55, 88, 89

values, 11, 18, 30, 36, 69, 71, 74

GPSR Compliance
The European Union's (EU) General Product Safety Regulation (GPSR) is a set of rules that requires consumer products to be safe and our obligations to ensure this.

If you have any concerns about our products, you can contact us on

ProductSafety@springernature.com

In case Publisher is established outside the EU, the EU authorized representative is:

Springer Nature Customer Service Center GmbH
Europaplatz 3
69115 Heidelberg, Germany

www.ingramcontent.com/pod-product-compliance
Lightning Source LLC
LaVergne TN
LVHW041956060526
838200LV00002B/37